Snowball Quilts

Cool Designs from an Easy Block

TAMMY KELLY

Martingale®
& COMPANY

MISSION STATEMENT

Dedicated to providing quality products and service to inspire creativity.

CREDITS

President ✦ Nancy J. Martin
CEO ✦ Daniel J. Martin
COO ✦ Tom Wierzbicki
Publisher ✦ Jane Hamada
Editorial Director ✦ Mary V. Green
Managing Editor ✦ Tina Cook
Technical Editor ✦ Laurie Baker
Copy Editor ✦ Sheila Chapman Ryan
Design Director ✦ Stan Green
Illustrator ✦ Laurel Strand
Cover and Text Designer ✦ Regina Girard
Photographer ✦ Brent Kane

Snowball Quilts: Cool Designs from an Easy Block
© 2007 by Tammy Kelly

That Patchwork Place® is an imprint
of Martingale & Company®.

Martingale & Company
20205 144th Ave. NE
Woodinville, WA 98072-8478 USA
www.martingale-pub.com

Printed in China
12 11 10 09 08 07   8 7 6 5 4 3 2 1

Library of Congress Cataloging-in-Publication Data
Library of Congress Control Number: 2006020285

ISBN: 978-1-56477-696-9

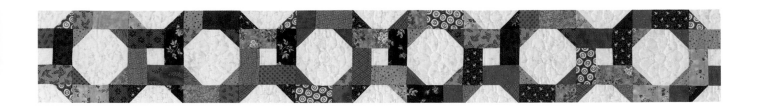

Dedication

To my family and greatest supporters, Dave and Lynnae

Acknowledgments

- ✦ The staff members at Martingale & Company for their vote of confidence
- ✦ Heidi Kaisand and the staff at American Patchwork and Quilting for selecting many of my projects for publication
- ✦ Alan Petersen for encouraging me to teach at Coconino Community College, and all my students who will pass on the quilting tradition
- ✦ Jay Inge and Tom Alexander who give my pattern line, Common Threads, a professional image with their graphics and photography
- ✦ Odegaards Sewing Center, Pine Country Quilts, and the Quilter's Store in Sedona for supporting local designers and willingly displaying my quilt samples
- ✦ Machine quilter Cydne Walker for her dependability
- ✦ Machine quilter Linda DeVries for her creativity and ability to make my quilts look like works of art
- ✦ Hand quilter Loralie Martin for her traditional tiny stitches
- ✦ My mom, Barbara Carlson, for her notes of encouragement
- ✦ My sister Natalie Carlson who always says "I'm proud of you"
- ✦ My sister Shelley Donnelly. Someday each of her three daughters will get her own quilt.
- ✦ My daughter, Lynnae Kelly, who has grown up with quilts
- ✦ My husband, Dave Kelly, who has stopped counting the number of quilts I've made

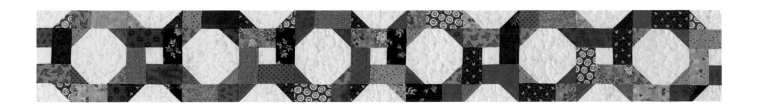

Contents

Just One More

Pink Lemonade

Sherbet Parfait

It Talked to Me

Wings of a Dragonfly

Snowballs and Spools

Ring around the Posies

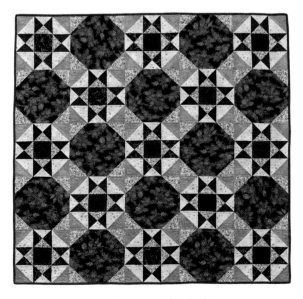

Marching Band in the Pines

Introduction

Making quilts with Snowball blocks can be absolutely addictive. Use my time-saving methods to construct the blocks and then arrange them in a variety of ways to create different looks. In this book, there are eight projects that use Snowball blocks in various sizes, along with connecting blocks that create secondary patterns. In addition, fabric-selection tips are included with each project to assist you in choosing fabrics that will create a dynamic quilt.

Because designing Snowball-block quilts is so fascinating, I've also given you information in "Fabric Selection" (page 7) for using color and value so that you can see what develops when the placement of light and dark fabric is changed. Once you get through this section, you should be more comfortable choosing fabrics and designing your own quilts. I've also included line drawings of each quilt in the book so you can use colored pencils to experiment with your own color choices.

Using connecting blocks can also change your quilt design. You can see how different the quilts in this book look just by partnering the Snowball blocks with a different block. Many block combinations create a secondary design. Of course, there are many more blocks other than the ones I've used that work well with the Snowball block. Be sure to read through "Connecting Blocks" (page 10) to get ideas on incorporating your own favorite block into your Snowball-block quilts.

The method I use for making Snowball blocks creates leftover triangles. Several of the projects use these triangles to create blocks that I've designed specifically for the borders. You can also use them to make an entirely different project. Follow the instructions in "Leftover Triangle Pairs" (page 11) for more information.

In "Quilting Basics" (page 12), I explain the methods I used throughout the creation process, from piecing through quilt completion. As you become a more confident quilter, you will learn that there are many ways to complete the same task. I encourage you to try new techniques and use the methods that produce the most gratifying results.

Whatever project you choose, make it your own, whether you change the color, the connecting block, or the border treatment. Break loose and have a great time with Snowball quilts!

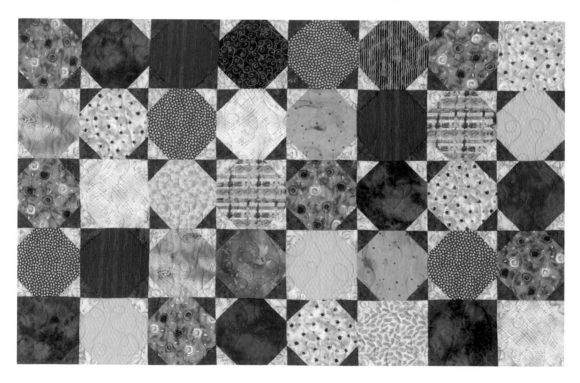

Fabric Selection

Many quilters find that the fabric selection process is their greatest challenge. This is the aspect of quilting I love the most. However, I do spend a considerable amount of time choosing fabrics. It's not uncommon for me to spend a couple of hours at the fabric shop making my initial selection for a project and then go home and make additional changes by incorporating pieces from my own stash.

I prefer using many fabrics. For example, in "It Talked to Me" (page 37), I could have used just one green fabric in the Snowball-block corners. Instead, I chose four different green fabrics which added more visual interest. I chose several different black fabrics for the connecting blocks of "Marching Band in the Pines" (page 46) for the same reason.

A variety of green fabrics

People often ask how much they should get when they come across a fabric they like but don't have a specific project in mind. My answer is ⅓ to ½ yard. This may seem less than what you'd imagine, but I prefer using a lot of *different* fabrics instead of a lot of the *same* fabrics. Now, if it's a focus fabric, I may purchase 1½ yards so that I have enough for the border. However, I rarely purchase more than that. This philosophy also keeps my stash to a minimum. I like to use up what I have and buy new stuff. I am amazed at what the fabric companies are producing and I want fresh fabric! I do shop often and buy a little piece of this and that—which is really fun! If you're concerned about running out of fabric, don't be. I think the most exciting projects are made when we have to make do and restructure our original plan.

When I'm shopping for fabric, I always let the fabric talk to me. If it doesn't talk to me, I don't buy it! When I find a bolt I like, I lay my fingers on the fabric so they form a square or triangle; that way I can see how the fabric will look when cut up into smaller pieces.

Of course, I tend to gravitate toward the fabrics that I like, such as batiks. Batiks tend to be priced a little higher than printed cloth, so I'm careful about spending, but again, I usually only get ½ yard so it isn't a large expenditure. I love the dyed variances in batiks—they never fail me!

I also enjoy fabrics with an unusual pattern. Spirals, coils, and swirls all have movement which I feel enhance my designs. Stripes can also be counted on for outstanding results. You can see the effects of a uniquely striped

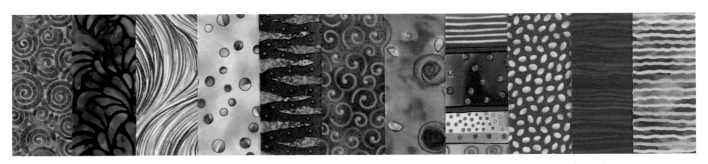

Stripes and geometrics create movement and excitement.

fabric in the extraordinary border of "Pink Lemonade" (page 31). Brights and metallics are also good choices and will almost always produce something outstanding.

I try to avoid being too "matchy" when I am selecting fabrics for a specific project. The nicely displayed coordinates are a great temptation. However, I have found that I am often disappointed with the results from a project that is too coordinated. Somehow the spark that I am looking for just doesn't happen when the project is completed. Sometimes I begin with the focus fabric because it is often made up of many colors. This enables me to find other fabrics that match with it. I like to vary the pattern and scale in the fabrics, such as a small print, a medium print, dots, and swirls. Tone-on-tone blender fabrics are necessary so the eye has a place to rest as it travels across the quilt. Other times I simply begin with a fabric that I really like and then go from there. Once I've selected several fabrics that I think will work well together, I enjoy asking the experienced clerks for their personal impressions. Sometimes they will make suggestions I hadn't considered. I often look at the choices from a distance and sometimes I squint at them to block out any outside factors. As you can imagine, this all takes time. There are occasions when I regret the choices I've made; however, I see every project as a learning experience so I don't concern myself with "messing up."

Value, which is the degree of lightness or darkness in a color, should be considered when gathering your fabrics. "Snowballs and Spools" (page 42) is a classic example of a lesson in selecting fabrics based on value. When designing this quilt, I wanted the spools to stand out yet blend into the Snowball blocks, so I grouped the medium-value fabrics that I selected for the snowball centers with the dark-value fabrics chosen for the spools. The light-value fabrics were strategically placed in the Nine Patch blocks to form the diagonally striped lines. You can see the individual fabrics that I used at right.

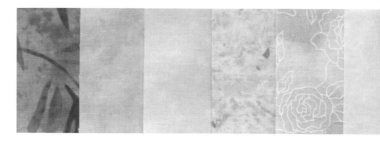

Light-value fabrics

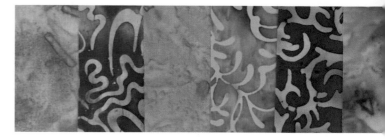

Medium-value fabrics

Dark-value fabrics

As you can see in "Snowballs and Spools," the secondary designs created by combining a Snowball block with another block will largely depend on where you decide to place the light, medium, and dark value fabrics. Be sure to experiment with the design sheets that are provided for each pattern. This will assist you in developing confidence in making fabric and color substitutions.

The Snowball Block

The finished Snowball blocks for the projects in this book vary in size from 5¾" to 12" square. There are various ways to construct a Snowball block; however, I prefer to use the folded-corners technique because I find that this is the simplest and easiest way to construct the blocks. Also, this method provides leftover triangles that can be incorporated into other parts of the quilt, such as the pieced borders that are featured in several of the projects.

To determine the size of the square needed for the Snowball-block corners, take a look at the connecting block and determine how it can be evenly divided. For example, a 9" finished Nine Patch block can be evenly divided into three 3" squares. Cut the corner squares 3" plus seam allowances, or 3½". If you are using just Snowball blocks in your quilt, calculate the corner squares at ⅓ the size of the finished block plus seam allowances. For the projects in this book, the approximate sizes for the corner squares will be given in the cutting instructions, so no additional calculations are required.

Each Snowball block has four corners, so you will need to cut four squares for the triangle corners.

To make a Snowball block, follow these instructions.

1. Fold and press each corner square in half diagonally, wrong sides together. This makes a crease that will be your sewing line. If you prefer, you can mark a diagonal line on the wrong side of each square with a water-soluble marker.

Fold in half or mark line.

2. With right sides together, open the squares and place one in each corner of the larger square that will be the snowball. Be sure the crease or marked line of each square is oriented in the direction shown. I don't find it necessary to pin down the corner squares, but you can if you'd like.

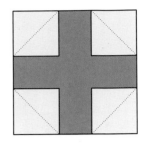

Corner square placement

3. Sew on the crease or marked line of each corner square. To expedite the process, turn the large square after sewing each corner without cutting the threads.

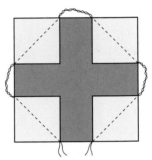

Sew on fold lines.

4. After you have attached all four corner squares, press the top of the Snowball block and trim the loose threads between the squares. Trim ¼" away from each seam using a ruler and rotary cutter for accuracy. Set aside the pairs of triangles that were trimmed away from each corner. Keep these triangle pairs together and use them for a pieced border or a future project (see "Leftover Triangle Pairs" on page 11). Press open the attached triangle in each corner to complete the Snowball block.

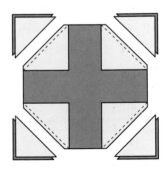

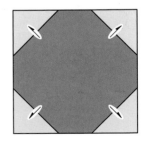

Snowball block

Connecting Blocks

The eight projects featured in this book provide you with opportunities to pair the Snowball block with Nine Patch, Fifty-Four Forty or Fight, Friendship Star, Road to California, Ohio Star, and Bright Hopes blocks.

These traditional patterns serve as excellent examples of connecting blocks because they create a secondary design when combined with the Snowball blocks. The resulting secondary design will depend on your fabric and value choices, as you can see in the illustration.

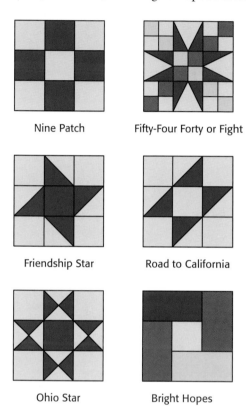

Nine Patch   Fifty-Four Forty or Fight

Friendship Star   Road to California

Ohio Star   Bright Hopes

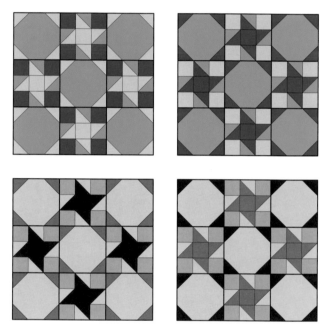

Various color layouts of the Snowball
and Friendship Star blocks

Use the design sheets that follow each project to further assist you with color placement. Feel free to explore other connecting blocks and design your own quilts.

Leftover Triangle Pairs

Once the quilt center is completed, it's fun to explore the possibilities for using the leftover triangle pairs that were created when you trimmed the Snowball-block corner squares. Consider using them to create additional blocks or borders, or to embellish a quilt label. Follow the instructions in "Chain Sewing" (page 14) to chain sew the pairs of triangles together to make half-square-triangle units; trim them to a uniform size.

Once the units are trimmed, experiment with various ideas to see what may enhance your quilt. "Just One More" (page 20), "Sherbet Parfait" (page 26), and "Ring around the Posies" (page 56) are examples of quilts that use half-square-triangle units in the borders. More ideas are given below. The units will vary in size depending on the dimensions of the Snowball block, so keep this in mind when planning your pieced border.

Half-square-
triangle unit

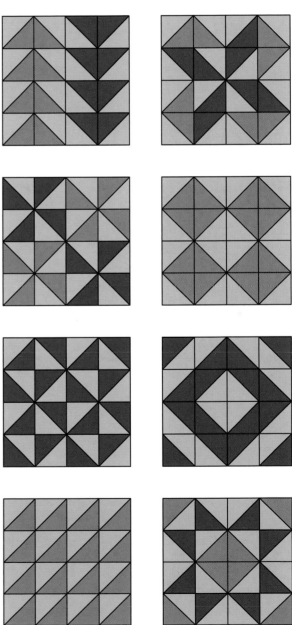

Quilting Basics

In recent years, experienced quilters have become much more sophisticated in their approach to quilting. The diverse selection of fabrics, tools, and machines available to quilters today is simply amazing. When I teach beginning and intermediate quilters, I try to show them a variety of ways to complete a task and let them choose the method that suits them best. People do become comfortable with one technique; however, I encourage them to be knowledgeable about alternative methods so they aren't dependent on one specific tool or supply. I also encourage my students to periodically stop and check for accuracy before repeatedly making the same errors and feeling frustrated as a result.

The instructions provided in the following pages are what produce good results for me. Whenever I work on a quilting project, I set a goal to enjoy the process, learn from the experience, and produce a high-quality quilt that will be treasured for years to come. I also encourage my students to take the time to apply their best effort to all aspects of quiltmaking. After all, we are creating heirlooms. Accuracy in cutting and piecing will make a big difference. Save yourself time by using proven techniques and tools. And remember, the seam ripper is your friend.

ROTARY CUTTING

Quilters need to understand fabric grain before they cut their fabrics. The lengthwise and crosswise grains are considered the straight of grain. Bias strips are made when the fabric is cut diagonally through the straight of grain. Cut the ends of border and binding strips on the bias so the seams are less noticable after they are joined together.

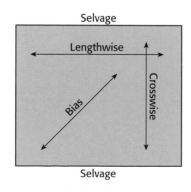

Fabric grain lines

All the pieces for the projects in this book are cut using rotary-cutting techniques. I use the lines on a cutting mat and a 6" x 24" ruler to assist me in cutting accurately. Begin with fabric that has been pressed. To cut crosswise strips, fold the fabric so that the selvages meet. Lay the fabric on the cutting mat with the folded edge toward you. Fold the fabric again toward the selvage, but not all the way to the selvage. This allows you to see the selvage to make sure it remains straight, and you will not have to stretch your arm across the whole width of the fabric when cutting. Place the folded edge along any horizontal line on the mat. Place the ruler on top of the fabric along the right edge, aligning a line of the ruler with the fabric fold. The raw, uneven edges should extend beyond the ruler's edge. Place your hand firmly on the ruler and trim off the end of the fabric to make a straight edge.

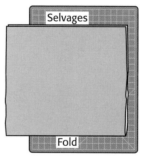

Fabric folded once

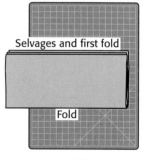

Fabric folded twice

Now, turn the fabric around and place the straightened edge to your left. Cut strips the width given in the project instructions, measuring from the straight edge. For example, if you need a 2½"-wide strip, place the 2½" line of the ruler on the straightened edge of the fabric and cut along the right edge of the ruler.

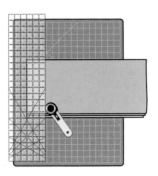

To cut squares and rectangles from a strip, unfold the cut strip once so that it is folded in half. Place the selvage edges to your right and make a cut, removing the selvages as you did for the fabric piece. Place the straightened edges to your left. Align the proper measurement on your ruler with the straightened end of the strip and cut the fabric into squares or rectangles.

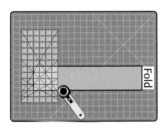

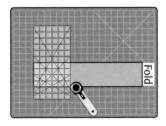

To make half-square triangles, cut the squares once diagonally. To make quarter-square triangles, cut the squares twice diagonally.

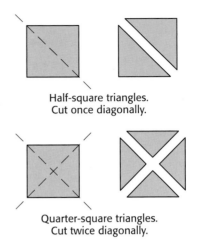

Half-square triangles.
Cut once diagonally.

Quarter-square triangles.
Cut twice diagonally.

MAKING AND CUTTING STRIP SETS

Some blocks are made by sewing strips of fabric together to make strip sets, and then cutting the strip sets into segments. The segments are sewn together in a particular order to make the blocks. To make the strip sets, sew together the strips indicated in the project instructions along the long edges. Press the seam allowances in the direction indicated. Straighten one end of the strip set, and then cut the required number of segments in the width indicated. You may need to restraighten the edge periodically.

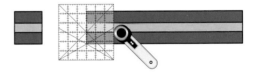

CHAIN SEWING

When feasible, I chain sew to decrease the time spent pulling the pieces away from the sewing machine and to reduce the amount of thread used to sew pieces together. Chain sewing is when you feed pairs of pieces under the presser foot one after the other without lifting the presser foot or clipping the connecting threads. When you are finished feeding all the pieces through, clip the threads between the units and press them as indicated in the project instructions.

JOINING BLOCKS

All the projects require accurate ¼" seam allowances so the pieces fit together properly. This is especially true when joining the Snowball blocks to other blocks—accuracy is required so that the seams line up and the points remain intact.

When you are sewing blocks together, begin by inserting a pin through the back of the Snowball block, ¼" away from the edge of a corner-square seam, as shown.

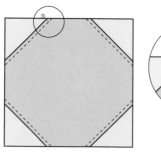 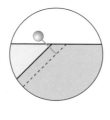

With right sides together, insert the point of the same pin through the corresponding seam of the adjoining block, ¼" away from the edge.

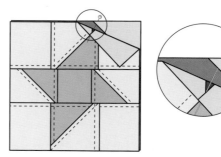

Hold the blocks together, being careful not to shift the fabric layers, and then place a pin on each side of the alignment pin. Repeat for the remaining corresponding seams on the edge that is being sewn together. Sew the blocks together, easing as necessary. After the blocks are sewn together, look on the right side to see if the points where the blocks join are accurate and intact.

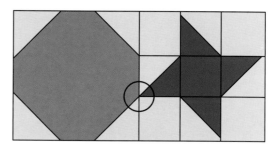

Connecting corner triangles form points.
Adjoining block points are intact.

If the points do not meet, remove a few stitches in the seam and resew it. To achieve an overall look of quality, it is worth the effort to correct any unsatisfactory seams.

PRESSING

Pressing is another aspect of quiltmaking that can make a big difference in the final outcome. Some quilters prefer using spray starch on their fabric. I do not use starch because I don't like the buildup on my iron or the stiffness it gives the fabric. I do recommend using a quality iron on a cotton setting with steam.

Before you begin pressing, consider the direction in which the seam allowances will be pressed. Adjoining seams should be pressed in opposite directions to reduce bulk and maintain accuracy. When possible, press toward the darker fabric.

When you have determined the pressing direction, place the piece on the ironing surface with the wrong side of the fabric that you want the seam allowance to be pressed toward facing up. Press directly on the seam line of the piece while it is in the closed position. This sets the seam and helps prevent distortion.

Next, open up the piece and glide the iron along the seam. This will automatically press the seam allowance toward the fabric that is on top.

Press the seam.

Finger-pressing can be a timesaver; however, I do not encourage you to take pressing shortcuts. Use finger-pressing techniques only when it's recommended in the instructions and doesn't interfere with the quality of a finished block.

BORDERS

The projects in this book provide examples of borderless quilts, quilts with simple borders, and quilts with pieced borders. All alternatives are acceptable in quiltmaking. Border strips are often used to frame a quilt. Ask yourself, when choosing borders for a quilt, if you want to draw attention to the quilt center or to the pieced borders. Regardless of the type of borders you apply to your quilt, your aim should be for a quilt that hangs straight and lies flat. Once the pieced center is completed, you are ready to audition fabrics for borders.

The dimensions provided in the quilt instructions for the borders are mathematically correct *if* the cutting, piecing, and pressing were done accurately. Adjustments are often necessary, so *do not cut your border strips the specified length until you have measured your own quilt.*

To determine the length to cut your side borders, carefully measure the length of the quilt center in three places. If the measurements are not all the same, average them. For example, if the three measurements are 29½", 29", and 29¼", the average would be 29¼". Cut two strips the length determined for the side borders.

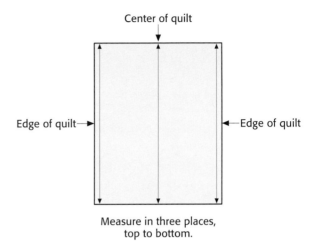

Measure in three places, top to bottom.

Pin mark the center of the quilt sides. Fold each border strip in half to find the center and gently crease. Match the centers and ends of the side borders and quilt; pin the borders to the sides, and then sew them in place. Press the seam allowances toward the borders unless otherwise instructed.

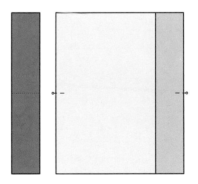

Pin the border center edge to the quilt center edge.

Measure the width of the quilt in three places (including the just-added borders) and determine the average. Cut two border strips to this measurement. Mark the centers of the border strips and the top and bottom edges of the quilt top as before. Pin the borders in place, matching the centers and ends, and sew them in place. Press the seam allowances toward the borders unless otherwise instructed.

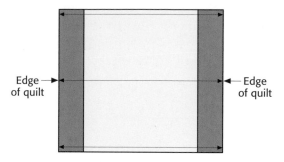

Measure in three places side to side.

Press the entire quilt. Use a square ruler to check each corner to make sure the quilt top is square. If the corners are not square, you will end up with a quilt that hangs very poorly and looks distorted. If needed, trim any slivers of fabric that are not within the squared corner.

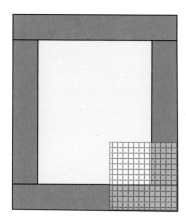

Once the quilt top is complete, take some time to clip away thread tails and fabric ears. Check for any twisted seams and make sure all the seams are pressed in the direction you intended. Re-press the entire front of the quilt. This will ensure that bulky seams or threads will not interfere with the quality of your quilting.

BACKING

The backing should be 4" to 6" larger than the quilt top. In some cases you will need to piece the backing fabric to make a piece large enough. I often make pieced backings from smaller pieces of fabric, merely to use up leftovers and avoid purchasing yardage. I randomly select pieces of fabric that coordinate with the front of the quilt and then sew them together until I have a backing that is large enough. Consider where the seams will be when you piece the backing. Avoid making a center seam, which puts undue stress down the middle of the quilt.

BATTING

Many quilters enjoy selecting specific battings for their quilts depending on how the quilt will be used and the overall desired appearance. I use a medium-loft, high-quality cotton batting from Quilters Dream for almost all my projects. This product is exceptional for both hand and machine quilting.

ASSEMBLING THE LAYERS

If you plan to quilt by hand or on your home sewing machine, the quilt top, batting, and backing will need to be layered and basted together. This process does not need to be followed if you plan on hiring a long-arm quilter, but there may be other requirements you should be aware of, so be sure to check with her before you deliver the quilt top.

To baste, spread the backing on a large, flat surface, wrong side up. Secure it with masking tape. The backing should be taut but not stretched. Center the batting over the backing, smoothing out any wrinkles. Center the quilt top on the batting, right side up. Smooth out any wrinkles.

For hand quilting, baste the layers together with thread, starting at the center and working toward each corner in an X shape. Then make a grid of horizontal and vertical lines no more than 6" apart. Finish by basting around the outside edges.

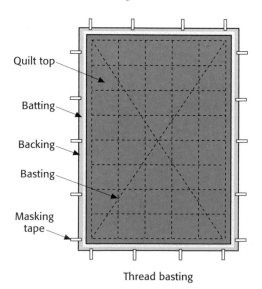

Quilt top

Batting

Backing

Basting

Masking tape

Thread basting

For machine quilting, baste the layers with No. 2 rustproof safety pins placed 3" to 4" apart.

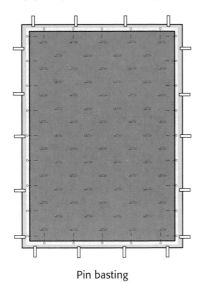

Pin basting

QUILTING

I have found the hand or machine quilting process to be the most labor-intensive part of the quiltmaking experience; therefore, I prefer to take advantage of the long-arm quilting experts in my area. This allows me the opportunity to spend my time on fabric selection, planning, and piecing my designs (not to mention writing). I have evolved into a "topper," mainly due to the extraordinary talents of my machine quilters. I am so confident in my quilters' abilities, I give them total rein when they machine quilt my projects. I have also been fortunate to have two friends who hand quilt for me when I have a very special project.

If you choose to hand or machine quilt your own project, choose high-quality threads and batting and consider quilting designs that will enhance the quilt. Take a class to learn hand or machine quilting before you tackle a family heirloom. A class will also help you develop expertise and confidence. Allow yourself adequate lighting and plenty of time to do your best. You do not need an elaborate design, but make sure you quilt evenly so that the line spacing is uniform across most of the quilt.

I enjoy free-motion designs that provide movement across the quilt that is different from the pieced blocks. For example, all the projects in this book have pieced squares and triangles; consequently, curved quilting designs provide a contrast that encourages the eye to travel over the quilt. The quilting should enhance the quilt, not detract from it.

Once the quilting is completed, take time to check the corners. If they need to be squared, used the same method explained in "Borders" (page 15). Trim the backing and batting so they extend ¼" beyond the quilt. This will ensure that there is batting within the binding, which helps your quilt last longer.

BINDING

It's important to consider how you will finish your quilt. Adding a binding using professional techniques will ensure that your quilt is completed with quality. All the projects in this book have straight edges and can be bound with straight-grain crosswise-cut or lengthwise-cut strips. A small wall hanging doesn't need the bulk of a double fold, so I use a single-fold binding. However, crib and bed quilts will last longer with double-fold binding.

Double-Fold Binding

1. Cut the specified number of 2½" x 42" strips needed for your project. Cut both ends of each strip at a 45° angle, except for the beginning of the first strip and the end of the last strip. Join the strips into one continuous piece as shown, keeping the straight-cut ends at the beginning and end of the continuous strip. Press the seams to one side.

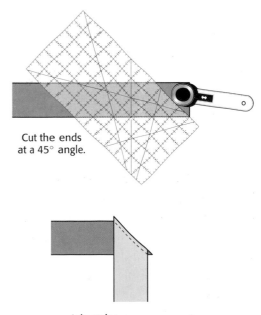

Cut the ends at a 45° angle.

Join strips.

2. Press the binding in half lengthwise, wrong sides together.

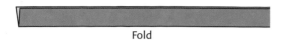

Fold

3. Place the binding on the front of the quilt several inches away from a corner, lining up the raw edge of the binding with the raw edge of the quilt. Using a ¼" seam allowance, stitch the binding to the quilt, beginning 3" away from the start of the binding and ending ¼" away from the first corner.

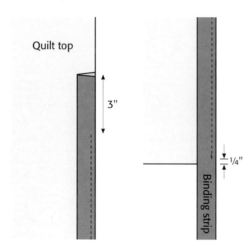

4. Remove the quilt from the sewing machine. Turn it so you are ready to sew the next edge. Fold the binding up away from the quilt at a 45° angle, and then fold it back down on top of itself. The fold should be even with the quilt top and the raw edges should be aligned. Begin stitching at the fold and continue stitching until you are ¼" from the next corner. Repeat the folding and stitching process at each corner as you work around the quilt.

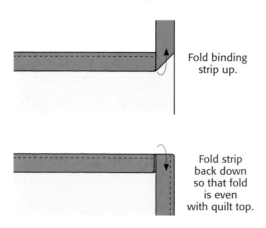

Fold binding strip up.

Fold strip back down so that fold is even with quilt top.

5. When you are approximately 3" away from the beginning of the binding, remove the quilt from the machine. Lap the end of the strip over the beginning of the strip. Trim both ends so they are ¼" longer than needed to meet.

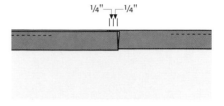

Trim ¼" longer on each end.

6. Unfold the strips and lift them away from the quilt. With right sides together, sew the ends together. Finger-press the seam open.

Stitch ends together.

7. Lay the binding back on the quilt, making sure it lies flat. Stitch the remaining portion of the binding to the quilt.

8. Turn the binding to the back of the quilt. Use thread that matches the binding to hand stitch the binding in place so that the folded edge covers the row of machine stitching. At each corner, fold the binding to form a miter on the back of the quilt.

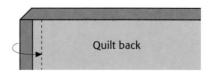

Quilt back

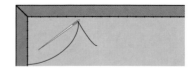

Hand stitch binding to quilt back.

Single-Fold Binding

1. Cut the specified number of 1½" x 42" strips needed for your project.

2. Refer to "Double-Fold Binding" (page 17) to cut the ends of each strip and join them together.

3. Press one long edge of the strip under ¼" to the wrong side.

4. Follow steps 3–8 of "Double-Fold Binding" to stitch the unpressed edge to the front of the quilt, and then hand stitch the folded edge to the back of the quilt.

LABELS

I encourage all quiltmakers to design a label for each quilt they make. A label should document the quilt name, the date it was made, the location where it was made, and the name of the quiltmaker and recipient. In addition, quilt care tips can be added and a personal story about the nature or purpose of the quilt can be shared.

A label can be made simply by using a piece of white or off-white prewashed cotton fabric and Sakura Pigma Micron permanent-ink pens. To stabilize the fabric, you may want to iron the shiny side of a piece of freezer paper to the back of the fabric to give it a firmer surface for you to work on. Write or illustrate the label with the pens; then remove the freezer paper from the backing.

To make printed labels, I prefer using June Tailor's computer printer fabric, which allows me to print labels on my home-computer printer. Type the contents of the label on the computer, and then print the fabric following the manufacturer's instructions. The fabric has a removable sticky backing to stabilize it. After it comes out of the printer, you can remove the backing. However, I have found the fabric to be very thin so I wait to remove the backing until after the borders have been sewn around the label.

To add borders to the label, cut strips from leftover fabric scraps. Sew a border strip around each side of the label just as you would with a quilt. Press the seams allowances away from the center. At this point, I remove the

paper backing and heat-set the printer ink with an iron. Cut a piece of backing fabric the same size as the pieced label. Place the label and backing right sides together and sew around the piece with a ¼" seam allowance. Trim the corners at an angle. Cut an X in the center of the backing fabric and turn the label inside out, pulling it through the hole. Pull out the corners so they are square.

Press the label flat. Hand stitch the raw edges of the X closed on the back of the label. Embellish the label with quilting if desired. Tack the label to the back of the quilt.

Just One More

Finished quilt size: 65" x 89"
Finished block size: 6" x 6"

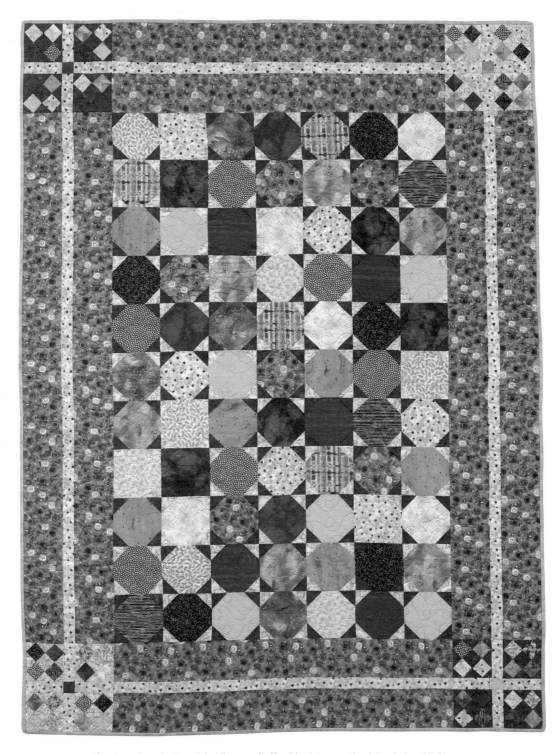

Designed and pieced by Tammy Kelly. Machine quilted by Cydne Walker.

*This quilt wasn't hard to name. After making many Snowball-block quilts with interconnecting blocks, I decided to do **just one more** quilt using only Snowball blocks. The 6" blocks in this project are great for utilizing scrap fabrics, and if you use brightly colored fabrics like I did, the Snowball blocks almost look like gumballs! The optional pieced border corners are made from the triangle pairs left over after making the Snowball blocks; they add interest without detracting from the quilt center.*

Fabric Selection Tips

I chose 13 medium to dark purple, green, blue, pink, and yellow fabric scraps for the Snowball blocks. Fabrics range from small- to medium-scale prints with an occasional blender fabric to rest the eye. To keep the juvenile theme, I chose bright fabrics with swirls, stripes, plaids, and dots. Light blue and dark blue corner triangles frame the snowballs. A fun, whimsical, medium-scale print was used for the border, with a yellow print adding another element that frames the quilt.

MATERIALS

Yardages are based on 42"-wide fabric.

⅓ yard *each* of 13 bright-colored fabrics for blocks

2⅞ yards of blue floral print for border

⅞ yard of dark blue fabric for blocks

⅞ yard of light blue fabric for blocks

⅝ yard of yellow print for border

⅔ yard of green fabric for binding

5¾ yards of fabric for backing

70" x 94" piece of batting

CUTTING

All measurements include ¼"-wide seam allowances. The cutting for the borders will be done later.

From the dark blue, cut:

✦ 10 strips, 2½" x 42"; crosscut into 156 squares, 2½" x 2½"

From the light blue, cut:

✦ 10 strips, 2½" x 42"; crosscut into 152 squares, 2½" x 2½"

From *each* of the 13 bright-colored fabrics, cut:

✦ 1 strip, 6½" x 42" (13 total); crosscut a random assortment of 77 squares, 6½" x 6½"

From the remainder of the bright-colored fabrics, cut a *total* of:

✦ 4 squares, 2" x 2"

From the yellow print, cut:

✦ 6 strips, 2" x 42"

✦ 16 pieces, 2" x 5½"

From the green, cut:

✦ 8 strips, 2½" x 42"

MAKING THE BLOCKS

1. Press the dark blue and light blue squares in half diagonally, wrong sides together.

2. Open each dark blue square and place one in each corner of a bright-colored 6½" square as shown, right sides together. Sew on the fold line of each corner square. Trim ¼" away from the seam using a rotary cutter and ruler to cut accurately. Set aside the cut-away triangle pairs for making the corner blocks, keeping the four pairs from each block together. Press open the attached triangle in each corner to complete the Snowball block. The block should measure 6½" square. Make a total of 39 blocks with dark blue corners. Repeat with the light blue squares to make a total of 38 blocks with light blue corners.

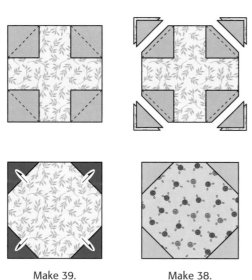

Make 39.   Make 38.

ASSEMBLING THE QUILT CENTER

1. Lay out the blocks in 11 rows of seven blocks each. Alternate the position of the blocks with dark corners and the blocks with light corners in each row and from row to row.

2. Sew the blocks in each row together. Press the seam allowances toward the blocks with dark corners.

3. Sew the rows together. Press the seam allowances in one direction. Press the entire quilt center. The pieced quilt center should measure 42½" x 66½".

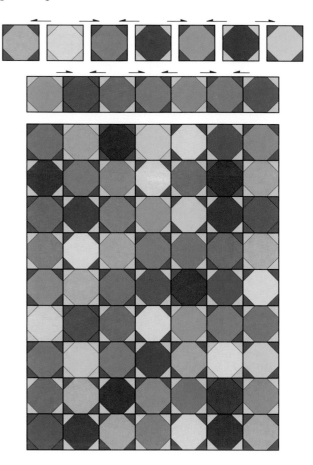

ASSEMBLING THE BORDER CORNER BLOCKS

1. From the triangle pairs that were set aside after trimming the corners of the Snowball blocks, select 32 sets of four matching triangle pairs with dark blue triangles (128 total) and 32 sets of four matching triangle pairs with light blue triangles (128 total).

2. Refer to "Leftover Triangle Pairs" (page 11) to chain sew the pairs of triangles together to make 256 half-square-triangle units. Press the seam allowances toward the blue fabric. Use a ruler and rotary cutter to trim each unit to 1¾" square.

Make 256.

3. Piece together four matching half-square-triangle units as shown. Press the seam allowances as indicated. Make 64 units.

Make 64.

4. Sew together four units with dark blue triangles from step 3 as shown. Press the seam allowances as indicated. Make eight. Repeat to make eight units with light blue triangles. The units should measure 5½" square.

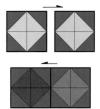

Make 8. Make 8.

5. Sew a yellow 2" x 5½" strip between two dark blue units from step 4. Press the seam allowances toward the yellow strip. Make four units with dark blue triangles and four units with light blue triangles.

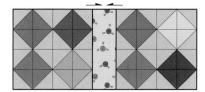

Make 4.

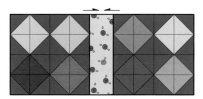

Make 4.

6. Sew a bright-colored 2" square between two yellow 2" x 5½" strips. Press the seam allowances toward the square. Make four.

Make 4.

7. Piece together the units from steps 5 and 6 to make two corner blocks with dark blue triangles and two corner blocks with light blue triangles. The blocks should measure 12" square.

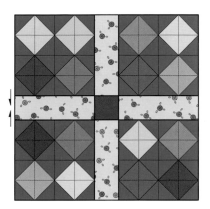

Make 2.

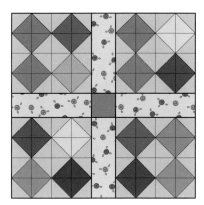

Make 2.

ASSEMBLING AND ADDING THE BORDERS

1. Refer to the diagram below to cut the blue floral 5½"-wide border strips.

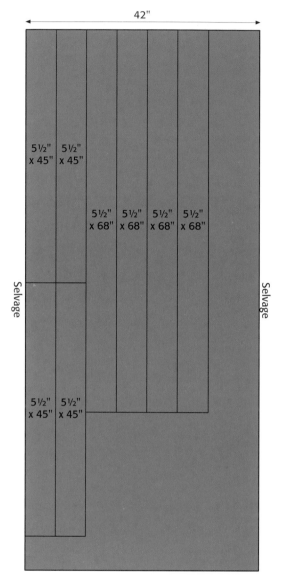

Border cutting diagram

2. Piece together the yellow 2"-wide strips end to end. From the pieced strip, cut two strips 68" long and two strips 45" long.

3. To make the side borders, sew a blue floral 68"-long strip to each side of the yellow 68"-long strips. Press the seam allowances toward the blue fabric. Measure the length of your quilt top and trim the two border-strip sets to the length measured.

4. To make the top and bottom borders, sew a blue floral 45"-long strip to each side of the yellow 45"-long strips. Press the seam allowances toward the blue fabric. Measure the width of your quilt top and trim the two border-strip sets to the length measured. Sew a dark blue corner block to one end of each strip and a light blue corner block to the opposite end. Press the seam allowances toward the border strip sets.

5. Sew the side borders to the quilt center. Press the seam allowances toward the borders. Sew the top and bottom borders to the quilt center as shown. Press the seam allowances toward the borders.

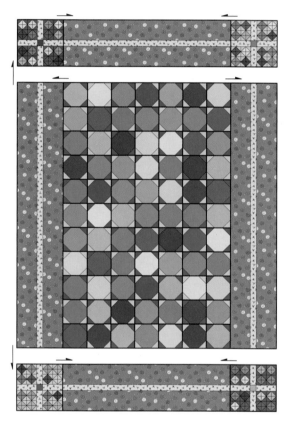

Quilt assembly

FINISHING THE QUILT

Refer to "Quilting Basics" (page 12) as needed to complete the following steps.

1. Layer the quilt top with the batting and backing. Baste the layers together.

2. Hand or machine quilt as desired.

3. Square up the quilt sandwich if needed.

4. Prepare and sew the binding to the quilt using the double-fold technique. Add a label.

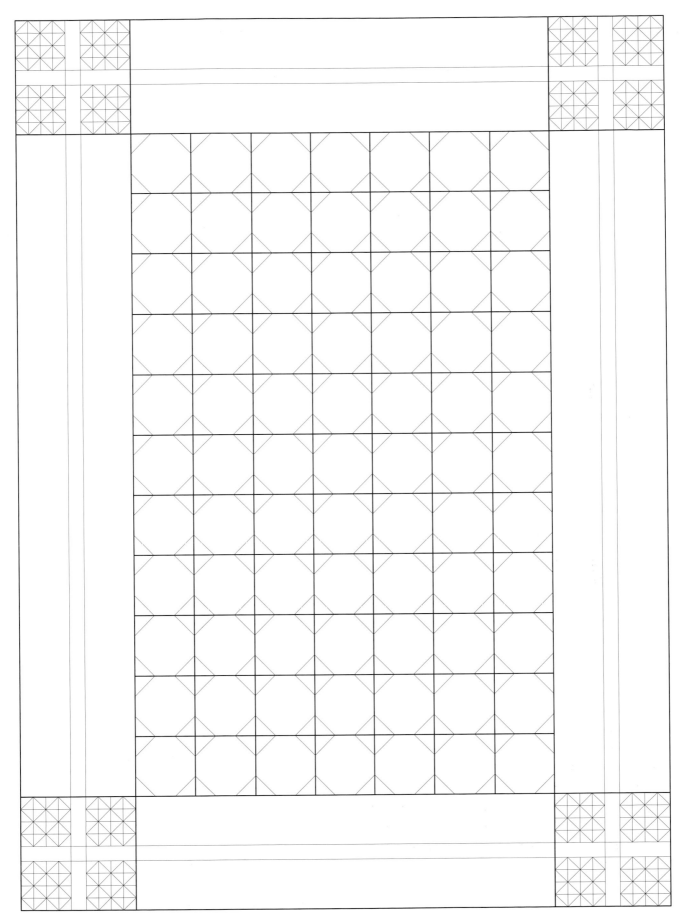

Sherbet Parfait

 Finished quilt size: 39" x 47½"
Finished block size: 6" x 6"

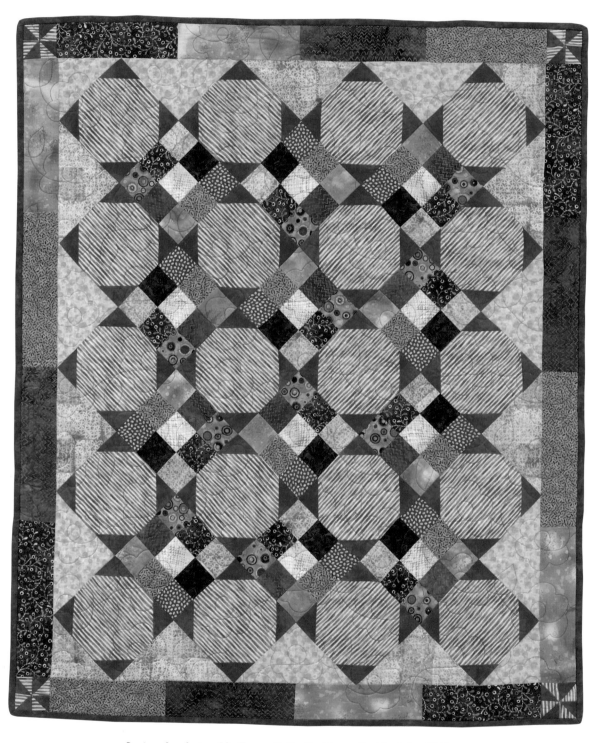

Designed and pieced by Tammy Kelly. Machine quilted by Cydne Walker.

Mix yummy fabrics and simple blocks together and you'll get delicious results! This recipe combines a 6" Snowball block with the basic Nine Patch block in a diagonal setting. The use of striped fabric creates an interesting pattern. The pieced border with pinwheel corners adds a finishing touch.

Fabric Selection Tips

All the fabric selections focus attention on the center of the blocks. The striped fabric in the Snowball blocks makes an intriguing impact on this traditional pattern. I chose a pink striped fabric with subtle green and yellow bits, which complements the various prints in the Nine Patch blocks. The Nine Patch blocks consist of pink (with a hint of orange), purple, yellow, and green squares from mostly small print and blender fabrics, and one medium print fabric. The purple was added so the finished quilt wasn't too pink. The green squares draw the eye to the center of the Nine Patch blocks. The corners of the Snowball blocks are made from a dark pink fabric, which creates a blended look, yet still separates the blocks. Yellow setting triangles complete the arrangement. The border is made up of fabrics left over from the quilt center.

MATERIALS

Yardages are based on 42"-wide fabric.

⅞ yard of pink striped fabric for Snowball blocks and border corner Pinwheel blocks

¼ yard *each* of 3 assorted pink prints for Nine Patch blocks and border

¼ yard *each* of 3 assorted purple prints for Nine Patch blocks and border

⅝ yard of yellow fabric for Nine Patch blocks and setting triangles

½ yard of dark pink fabric for Snowball blocks and border corner Pinwheel blocks

⅛ yard of lime green print for Nine Patch blocks

⅛ yard of orange-and-pink print for Nine Patch blocks

½ yard of purple for binding

2⅞ yards of fabric for backing

45" x 54" piece of batting

CUTTING

All measurements include ¼"-wide seam allowances.

From the dark pink, cut:

✦ 5 strips, 2½" x 42"; crosscut into 80 squares, 2½" x 2½"

From the pink striped fabric, cut:

✦ 4 strips, 6½" x 42"; crosscut into 20 squares, 6½" x 6½"

From *each* of the 3 assorted pink prints, cut:

✦ 1 strip, 2½" x 42" (3 total)

From the remainder of *each of 2* of the assorted pink prints, cut:

✦ 2 pieces, 3" x 11⅛" (4 total)
✦ 2 pieces, 3" x 9" (4 total)

From *each* of the 3 assorted purple prints, cut:

✦ 1 strip, 2½" x 42" (3 total)

From the remainder of *each of 2* of the assorted purple prints, cut:

✦ 2 pieces, 3" x 11⅛" (4 total)
✦ 2 pieces, 3" x 9" (4 total)

From the lime green print, cut:

✦ 1 strip, 2½" x 42"

From the orange-and-pink print, cut:

✦ 1 strip, 2½" x 42"

From the yellow, cut:

✦ 1 strip, 2½" x 42"

✦ 4 squares, 9¾" x 9¾"; cut twice diagonally to yield 16 side setting triangles (2 will be extra)

✦ 2 squares, 5⅛" x 5⅛"; cut once diagonally to yield 4 corner triangles

From the purple, cut:

✦ 5 strips, 2½" x 42"

MAKING THE BLOCKS

1. To make the Snowball blocks, press the dark pink 2½" squares in half diagonally, wrong sides together. Open each square and place one in each corner of a pink striped square as shown. Sew on the fold line of each corner square. Trim ¼" away from the seam using a rotary cutter and ruler to cut accurately. Set aside the cut-away triangle pairs for making the border corner blocks, keeping the pairs together. Press open the attached triangle in each corner to complete the Snowball block. The block should measure 6½" square. Repeat to make a total of 20 blocks.

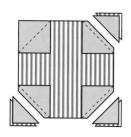

Make 20.

2. To make the Nine Patch blocks, sew together the pink, purple, lime green, orange-and-pink, and yellow 2½" x 42" strips as shown to make strip sets A, B, and C. Press the seam allowances in the directions indicated for each strip set. The strip sets should

measure 6½" wide. Crosscut each strip set into 12 segments, 2½" wide.

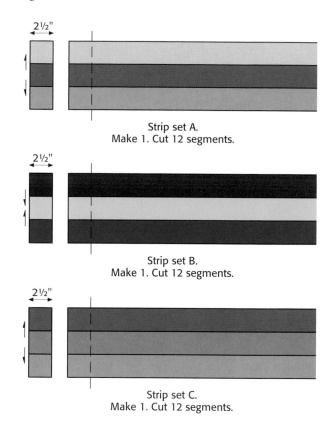

Strip set A.
Make 1. Cut 12 segments.

Strip set B.
Make 1. Cut 12 segments.

Strip set C.
Make 1. Cut 12 segments.

3. Lay out one segment from each strip set into three vertical rows as shown. Sew the segments together. Press the seam allowances away from the center segment to complete a Nine Patch block. The block should measure 6½" square. Repeat to make a total of 12 blocks.

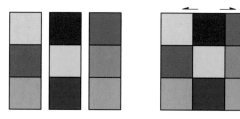

Make 12.

ASSEMBLING THE QUILT CENTER

1. Lay out the blocks and yellow side setting triangles in diagonal rows.

2. Sew together the blocks and side triangles in each row. Press the seam allowances toward the Nine Patch blocks and side triangles.

3. Sew the rows together, adding the yellow corner triangles last. Press the seam allowances in one direction. Press the entire quilt center.

4. Square up the quilt center, trimming the edges ¼" from the block corners as needed. The pieced quilt center should measure 34½" x 43".

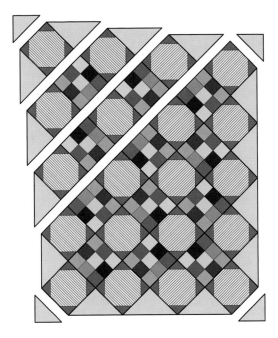

ASSEMBLING THE BORDER CORNER BLOCKS

1. Select 16 pairs of triangles that were set aside after trimming the corners of the Snowball blocks.

2. Refer to "Leftover Triangle Pairs" (page 11) to chain sew the pairs of triangles together to make 16 half-square-triangle units. Press the seam allowances toward the dark pink fabric. Use a ruler and rotary cutter to trim each unit to 1¾" square.

Make 16.

3. Sew together two half-square-triangle units to make a pair. Make eight pairs. Press the seam allowances in one direction. Join two pairs as shown to make a Pinwheel block. Press the seam allowance in one direction. Repeat to make a total of four Pinwheel blocks.

Make 8.   Make 4.

ASSEMBLING AND ADDING THE BORDERS

1. To make the side borders, sew together two purple and pink 3" x 11⅛" pieces end to end, alternating colors. Repeat to make a total of two side border strips. Sew the borders to the quilt center. Press the seam allowances toward the borders.

2. To make the top and bottom borders, sew together two purple and pink 3" x 9" pieces end to end, alternating colors. Repeat to make a total of two strips. Sew a Pinwheel block to both ends of each strip. Sew the borders to the quilt center as shown. Press the seam allowances toward the borders.

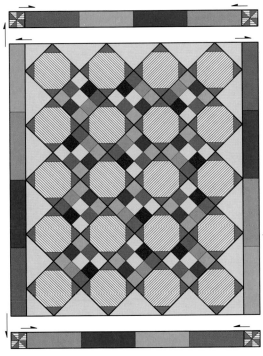

Quilt assembly

FINISHING THE QUILT

Refer to "Quilting Basics" (page 12) as needed to complete the following steps.

1. Layer the quilt top with the batting and backing. Baste the layers together.

2. Hand or machine quilt as desired.

3. Square up the quilt sandwich if needed.

4. Prepare and sew the binding to the quilt using the double-fold technique. Add a label.

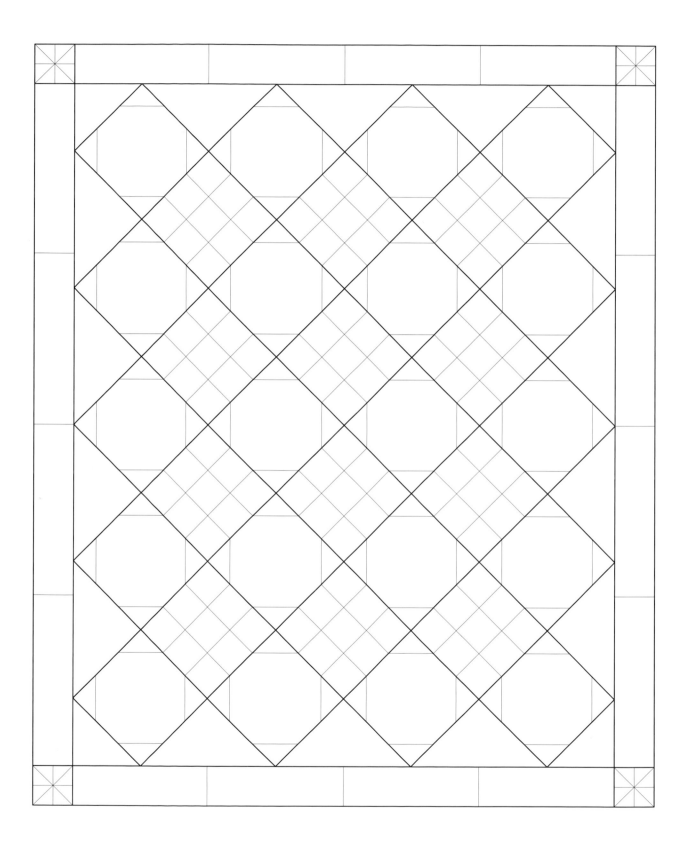

Pink Lemonade

Finished quilt size: 29½" x 29½"
Finished block size: 6" x 6"

Designed and pieced by Tammy Kelly. Machine quilted by Linda DeVries.

Create the illusion of curved piecing by combining the Snowball block with the historic Fifty-Four Forty or Fight block. Easy piecing and a simple setting make this small wall hanging quick to make, which means you'll soon be sipping a tall glass of the real pink lemonade and enjoying the fruits of your labor.

Fabric Selection Tips

I chose a light pink swirled batik to provide contrast in the quilt center. The corners of the Snowball blocks incorporate the same pink-and-orange large-scale sunflower print fabric that is used in the Fifty-Four Forty or Fight blocks. This makes the two blocks flow together as if they were one piece, creating the diagonal movement across the quilt. A marbled medium pink fabric was used for the star points to soften the contrast. The inner border pulls the quilt center together with its eye-catching geometric yellow-and-pink circles. The yellow batik used for the middle border separates the quilt center from the outer border. The outer border fabric is a pink striped batik that was fussy cut so that the dark shadows would fall around the perimeter of the quilt. The same fabric was used for the single-fold binding.

MATERIALS

Yardages are based on 42"-wide fabric.

¾ yard of pink striped batik for outer border and binding

½ yard of light pink swirled batik for blocks

⅜ yard of pink-and-orange large-scale sunflower print for blocks and border corners

⅛ yard of marbled medium pink fabric for Fifty-Four Forty or Fight blocks

⅛ yard of yellow batik for middle pieced border

⅛ yard of yellow-and-pink circle print for inner pieced border

1 yard of fabric for backing

36" x 36" piece of batting

Template plastic (optional)

CUTTING

All measurements include ¼"-wide seam allowances.

From the pink-and-orange print, cut:
✦ 1 strip, 2½" x 42"; crosscut into 16 squares, 2½" x 2½"
✦ 2 strips, 1½" x 42"
✦ 4 squares, 4¼" x 4¼"
✦ 9 squares, 2½" x 2½"

From the light pink batik, cut:
✦ 1 strip, 6½" x 42"; crosscut into 4 squares, 6½" x 6½"
✦ 2 strips, 1½" x 42"
✦ 2 strips, 2⅞" x 42"

From the medium pink, cut:
✦ 2 strips, 1¾" x 42". Fold the strips in half crosswise, right sides together; crosscut into 10 pairs of rectangles, 1¾" x 3¼". Keep the pairs together. Cut each pair once diagonally to yield 20 pairs of triangles. Keep the pairs together.

From the yellow-and-pink print, cut:
✦ 2 strips, 1½" x 42"; crosscut into 4 pieces, 1½" x 18½"

From the yellow batik, cut:
✦ 2 strips, 1½" x 42"; crosscut into 4 pieces, 1½" x 18½"

From the pink striped batik, cut:

- ✦ 4 strips, 4¼" x 42"; crosscut into 4 pieces, 4¼" x 22½"
- ✦ 3 strips, 1½" x 42"

MAKING THE BLOCKS

1. To make the Snowball blocks, press the pink-and-orange 2½" squares in half diagonally, wrong sides together. Open each square and place one in each corner of a light pink batik 6½" square as shown. Sew on the fold line of each corner square. Trim ¼" away from the seam using a rotary cutter and ruler to cut accurately. Set aside the cut-away triangle pairs for a future project. Press open the attached triangle in each corner to complete the Snowball block. The block should measure 6½" square. Repeat to make a total of four blocks.

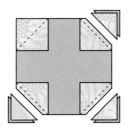

Make 4.

2. To make the Fifty-Four Forty or Fight blocks, sew each pink-and-orange 1½" x 42" strip to a light pink 1½" x 42" strip as shown to make two strip sets. Press the seam allowances toward the pink-and-orange strips. The strip sets should measure 2½" wide. Crosscut the strip sets into 40 segments, 1½" wide.

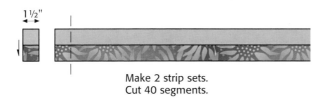

Make 2 strip sets.
Cut 40 segments.

3. Sew two segments together as shown to make a four-patch unit. Press the seam allowance in either direction. Repeat to make a total of 20 units.

Make 20.

4. Cut the star point pieces from the light pink 2⅞" x 42" strips using one of the following two options.

Option 1: Crosscut the strips into 20 squares, 2⅞" x 2⅞". Mark the center of the upper edge on each square. Use your rotary cutter and ruler to trim from the lower corners to the center point as shown. Discard the side pieces.

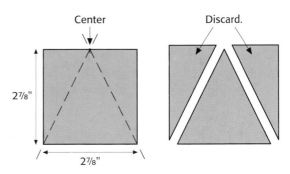

Option 2: Trace the triangle pattern (page 35) onto template plastic with a permanent pen and cut it out using your rotary cutter and ruler to cut accurately. Place the template on one end of the strip, aligning the bottom of the triangle with the bottom of the strip and the tip of the triangle with the top of the strip. Place your ruler along one side of the template, aligning the edges. Slide the template away and cut along the ruler edge. Repeat with the remaining side. Place the template on the strip again, reversing the template so that the tip is at the bottom of the strip and one side is aligned with the previously cut edge. Place your ruler on the template and cut out the shape as before. Continue doing this for the length of the strip. Repeat with the remaining strip to cut a total of 20 triangles.

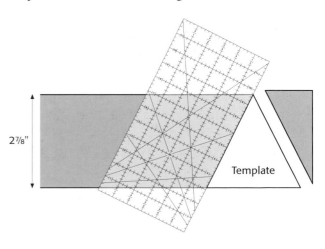

5. Using one pair of medium pink triangles, sew a triangle to one side of a just-cut light pink star point as shown. Press the seam allowance away from the center triangle. Sew the remaining medium pink triangle to the other side of the light pink center triangle as shown. Press the seam allowance away from the center triangle. Clip the fabric ears that extend beyond the square. Trim to 2½" square, if needed. Repeat to make a total of 20 star-point units.

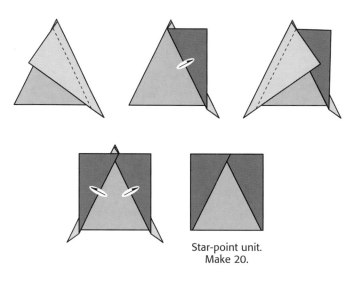

Star-point unit.
Make 20.

6. Lay out four four-patch units, four star-point units, and one pink-and-orange 2½" square into three horizontal rows as shown. Sew the units in each row together. Press the seam allowances away from the star-point units. Sew the rows together. Press the seam allowances away from the center. Repeat to make a total of five blocks.

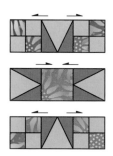
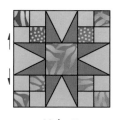

Make 5.

ASSEMBLING THE QUILT CENTER

1. Lay out the blocks in three horizontal rows of three blocks each. Alternate the position of the blocks in each row and from row to row.

2. Sew the blocks in each row together. Use pins as needed to make sure the corners match. Press the seam allowances toward the Snowball blocks.

3. Sew the rows together. Press the seam allowances in one direction. Press the entire quilt center. The pieced quilt center should measure 18½" square.

ASSEMBLING AND ADDING THE BORDERS

1. Sew each yellow-and-pink print 1½" x 18½" strip to a yellow batik 1½" x 18½" strip to make the inner- and middle-border strips. Press the seam allowances toward the yellow-and-pink strips. The border strips should measure 2½" x 18½". Sew border strips to the sides of the quilt center. Press the seam allowances toward the borders. Add pink-and-orange 2½" squares to both ends of the two remaining pieced border strips. Sew these strips to the top and bottom of the quilt center. Press the seam allowances toward the borders.

2. Sew pink striped 4¼" x 22½" strips to the sides of the quilt. Press the seam allowances toward the outer borders. Add pink-and-orange 4¼" squares to both ends of the remaining two pink striped 4¼" x 22½" strips. Sew these strips to the top and bottom of the quilt. Press the seam allowances toward the outer borders.

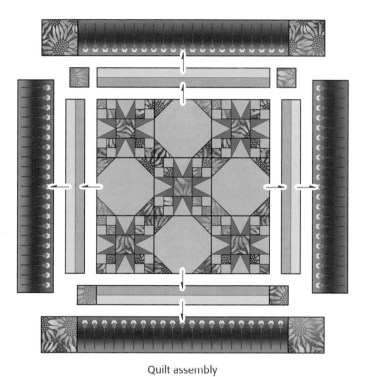

Quilt assembly

FINISHING THE QUILT

Refer to "Quilting Basics" (page 12) as needed to complete the following steps.

1. Layer the quilt top with the batting and backing. Baste the layers together.

2. Hand or machine quilt as desired.

3. Square up the quilt sandwich if needed.

4. Prepare and sew the binding to the quilt using the single-fold technique. Add a label.

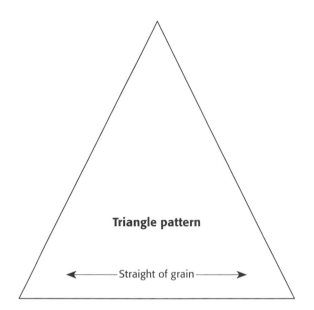

Triangle pattern

◄— Straight of grain —►

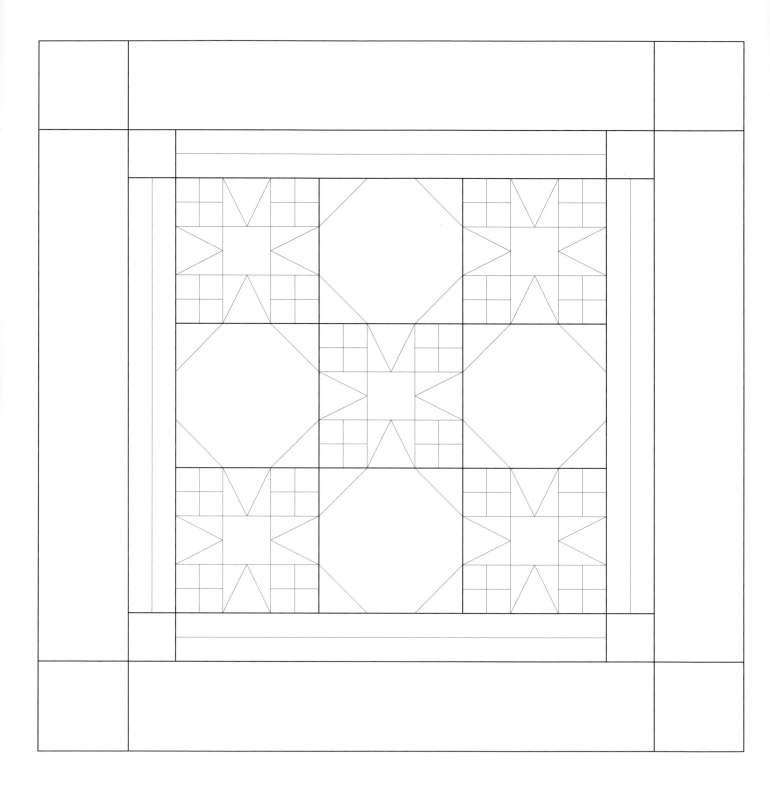

It Talked to Me

 Finished quilt size: 51½" x 51½"
Finished block size: 9" x 9"

Designed and pieced by Tammy Kelly. Machine quilted by Linda DeVries.

This bright orange floral print practically jumped off the shelf and said "Buy me"—so I just had to purchase it! The 9" Snowball blocks in this alluring wall hanging or crib-sized quilt work especially well with large-scale print fabrics, and combine beautifully with the Friendship Star blocks. A simple border draws the eye to the quilt center.

Fabric Selection Tips

I began with the large-scale floral print fabric and picked all my other fabrics based on the flower and leaf colors. I used four different green fabrics for the Snowball-block corners, which adds more interest than using just one fabric. Then I selected the bright yellow polka-dot print and sky blue fabric for the Friendship Star blocks. Interestingly, this quilt is made up of all medium-value fabrics. This is something I almost never do, because I prefer to make quilts with contrast; however, I think it works in this quilt because of the large flowers in the Snowball blocks. I tried using a busy fabric in the border, but it took away from the pieced center blocks, so I settled for simple borders made from yellow and blue blender fabrics.

MATERIALS

Yardages are based on 42"-wide fabric.

1⅝ yards of orange large-scale floral print for Snowball blocks

¼ yard *each* of 4 assorted green fabrics for Snowball blocks

⅝ yard of sky blue fabric for Friendship Star blocks

½ yard of yellow polka-dot print for Friendship Star blocks

½ yard of blue print for outer border

¼ yard of yellow fabric for inner border

½ yard of orange print for binding

3⅝ yards of fabric for backing

59" x 59" piece of batting

CUTTING

All measurements include ¼"-wide seam allowances.

From *each* of the 4 assorted greens, cut:
- ✦ 2 strips, 3½" x 42"; crosscut into 13 squares, 3½" x 3½" (52 total)

From the orange floral print, cut:
- ✦ 4 strips, 9½" x 42"; crosscut into 13 squares, 9½" x 9½"
- ✦ 3 strips, 3⅞" x 42"; crosscut into 24 squares, 3⅞" x 3⅞". Cut each square once diagonally to yield 48 triangles.

From the sky blue, cut:
- ✦ 3 strips, 3⅞" x 42"; crosscut into 24 squares, 3⅞" x 3⅞". Cut each square once diagonally to yield 48 triangles.
- ✦ 2 strips, 3½" x 42"; crosscut into 12 squares, 3½" x 3½"

From the yellow polka-dot print, cut:
- ✦ 5 strips, 3½" x 42"; crosscut into 48 squares, 3½" x 3½"

From the yellow for the inner border, cut:
- ✦ 5 strips, 1¼" x 42"

From the blue print for the outer border, cut:
- ✦ 5 strips, 3" x 42"

From the orange print for binding, cut:
- ✦ 6 strips, 2½" x 42"

MAKING THE BLOCKS

1. To make the Snowball blocks, press the green 3½" squares in half diagonally, wrong sides together. Open each square and place one in each corner of an orange floral 9½" square as shown. Sew on the fold line of each corner square. Trim ¼" away from the seam using a rotary cutter and ruler to cut accurately. Set aside the cut-away triangle pairs for a future project. Press open the attached triangle in each corner to complete the Snowball block. The block should measure 9½" square. Repeat to make a total of 13 blocks.

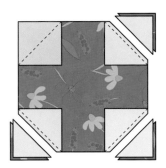

Make 13.

2. To make the Friendship Star blocks, sew each orange floral triangle to a sky blue triangle to make a half-square-triangle unit. Refer to "Chain Sewing" (page 14) to make the sewing process quicker, if desired. Press the seam allowances toward the darker fabric. Make 48.

Make 48.

3. Lay out four yellow polka-dot 3½" squares, four half-square-triangle units, and one sky blue 3½" square into three horizontal rows as shown. Sew the units in each row together. Press the seam allowances toward the blue and yellow squares. Sew the rows together.

Press the seam allowances away from the center row. Repeat to make a total of 12 blocks.

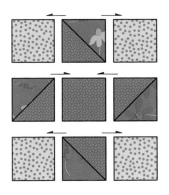

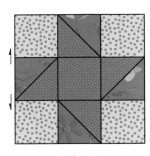

Make 12.

ASSEMBLING THE QUILT CENTER

1. Lay out the blocks in five horizontal rows of five blocks each. Alternate the position of the blocks in each row and from row to row.

2. Sew the blocks in each row together. Use pins as needed to make sure the corners match. Press the seam allowances toward the Snowball blocks.

3. Sew the rows together. Press the seam allowances in one direction. Press the entire quilt center. The pieced quilt center should measure 45½" square.

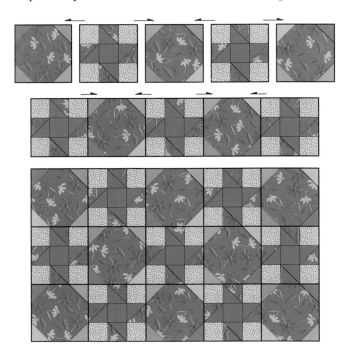

ADDING THE BORDERS

1. Piece together the yellow 1¼" x 42" strips end to end. From the pieced strip, cut two strips 45½" long for the inner side borders and two strips 47" long for the inner top and bottom borders. Sew the side borders to the quilt center. Press the seam allowances toward the border. Sew the top and bottom borders to the quilt center. Press the seam allowances toward the borders.

2. Piece together the blue print 3" x 42" strips end to end. From the pieced strip, cut two strips 47" long for the outer side borders and two strips 52½" long for the outer top and bottom borders. Sew the strips to the quilt top in the same manner as for the inner borders, pressing the seam allowances toward the outer borders after each addition.

FINISHING THE QUILT

Refer to "Quilting Basics" (page 12) as needed to complete the following steps.

1. Layer the quilt top with the batting and backing. Baste the layers together.

2. Hand or machine quilt as desired.

3. Square up the quilt sandwich if needed.

4. Prepare and sew the binding to the quilt using the double-fold technique. Add a label.

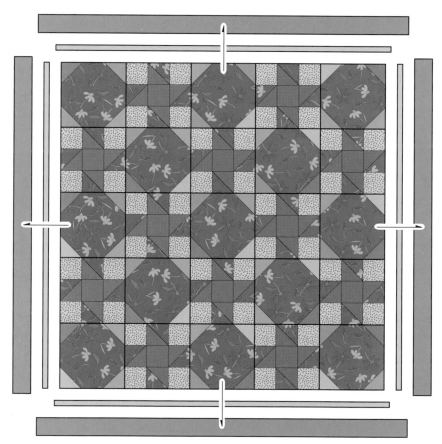

Quilt assembly

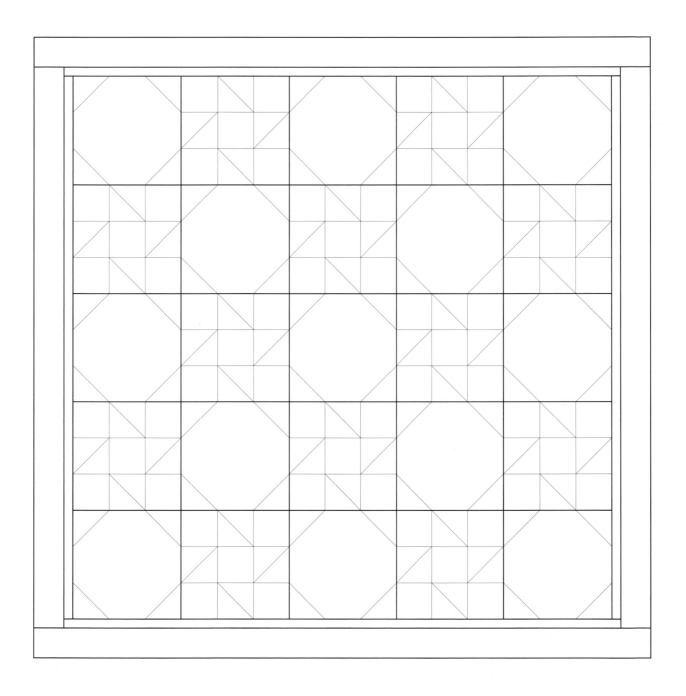

Snowballs and Spools

 Finished quilt size: 63" x 63"
Finished block size: 9" x 9"

Designed and pieced by Tammy Kelly. Machine quilted by Linda DeVries.

Light, medium, and dark fabric selections create an obvious diagonal pattern when the 9" Snowball block is combined with the Road to California block. This is an example of how the combination of two blocks made from carefully selected fabrics can make a secondary design. This large, scrappy wall hanging or sofa throw could easily be converted to any bed size by adding more blocks in either or both directions.

Fabric Selection Tips

This is an excellent project for using up your scrap fabrics. To achieve the effect of diagonal stripes, I chose very light blues, greens, and pinks that were almost white for the area that creates the stripe in the Road to California blocks. I selected printed fabrics for the lights because very light values are often difficult to obtain from batiks. Using many fabrics instead of one creates the appearance of a watercolor painting. The dark fabrics used in the corners of the Road to California blocks are also used in the corners of the Snowball blocks; this creates a spool design. Medium-value batik fabrics in pinks and blues are used for the Snowball centers. The medium- and dark-value fabrics are primarily batiks because I have a lot of small pieces in my collection and I enjoy the impact that they have on my quilts.

MATERIALS

Yardages are based on 42"-wide fabric.

¼ yard *each* of 8 assorted very light green, very light blue, and very light pink fabrics for Road to California blocks

⅜ yard *each* of 5 assorted dark pink fabrics for blocks

⅜ yard *each* of 5 assorted dark blue fabrics for blocks

⅓ yard *each* of 4 assorted medium pink fabrics for Snowball blocks

⅓ yard *each* of 3 assorted medium blue fabrics for Snowball blocks

⅝ yard of pink print for binding

3⅞ yards of fabric for backing

69" x 69" piece of batting

CUTTING

All measurements include ¼"-wide seam allowances.

From *each* of the 5 assorted dark pinks, cut:

✦ 2 strips, 3½" x 42" (10 total); crosscut a random assortment of 76 squares, 3½" x 3½"

From *each* of 3 of the assorted dark pinks, cut:

✦ 1 strip, 3⅞" x 42" (3 total)

From *each* of the 5 assorted dark blues, cut:

✦ 2 strips, 3½" x 42" (10 total); crosscut a random assortment of 72 squares, 3½" x 3½"

From *each* of 3 of the assorted dark blues, cut:

✦ 1 strip, 3⅞" x 42" (3 total)

From the 4 assorted medium pinks, cut a *total* of:

✦ 13 squares, 9½" x 9½"

From the 3 assorted medium blues, cut a *total* of:

✦ 12 squares, 9½" x 9½"

From *each* of the 8 assorted very light fabrics, cut:

✦ 1 strip, 3½" x 42" (8 total); crosscut a random assortment of 72 squares, 3½" x 3½"

From *each* of 6 of the assorted very light fabrics, cut:

✦ 1 strip, 3⅞" x 42" (6 total)

From the pink print, cut:

✦ 7 strips, 2½" x 42"

MAKING THE BLOCKS

1. To make the Snowball blocks, press 52 dark pink and 48 dark blue 3½" squares in half diagonally, wrong sides together.

2. Open each pressed dark pink square and place one in each corner of a medium pink 9½" square as shown. Sew on the fold line of each corner square. Trim ¼" away from the seam using a rotary cutter and ruler to cut accurately. Set aside the cut-away triangle pairs for a future project. Press open the attached triangle in each corner to complete the Snowball block. The block should measure 9½" square. Make a total of 13 pink Snowball blocks. Repeat with the dark blue 3½" squares and medium blue 9½" squares to make a total of 12 blue Snowball blocks.

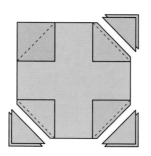

Make 13.

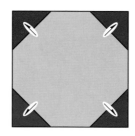

Make 12.

3. To make the Road to California blocks, pair each very light 3⅞" x 42" strip with an assorted dark pink or dark blue 3⅞" x 42" strip, right sides together. Make six pairs. Crosscut each pair into eight squares, 3⅞" x 3⅞" (48 total). Cut each pair of squares once diagonally to yield 96 triangle pairs. Keep the pairs together. Refer to "Leftover Triangle Pairs" (page 11) to chain sew the pairs together to make half-square-triangle units. Press the seam allowances toward the dark fabrics. Make 48 dark pink units and 48 dark blue units.

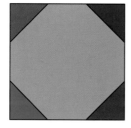

Make 48.   Make 48.

4. Lay out one dark pink 3½" square, one dark blue 3½" square, three very light 3½" squares, two dark pink half-square-triangle units, and two dark blue half-square-triangle units into three horizontal rows as shown. Sew the units in each row together. Press the seam allowances toward the squares. Sew the rows together. Press the seam allowances away from the center row. Repeat to make a total of 24 blocks.

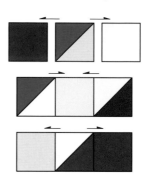
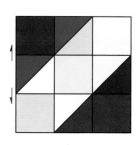

Make 24.

ASSEMBLING THE QUILT

1. Lay out the blocks in seven horizontal rows of seven blocks each. Alternate the position of the blocks in each row and from row to row.

2. Sew the blocks in each row together, making sure the corners match. Press the seam allowances toward the Snowball blocks.

3. Sew the rows together. Press the seam allowances in one direction. Press the entire quilt top.

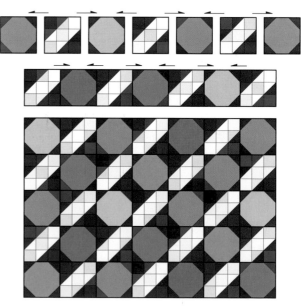

Quilt assembly

FINISHING THE QUILT

Refer to "Quilting Basics" (page 12) as needed to complete the following steps.

1. Layer the quilt top with the batting and backing. Baste the layers together.

2. Hand or machine quilt as desired.

3. Square up the quilt sandwich if needed.

4. Prepare and sew the binding to the quilt using the double-fold technique. Add a label.

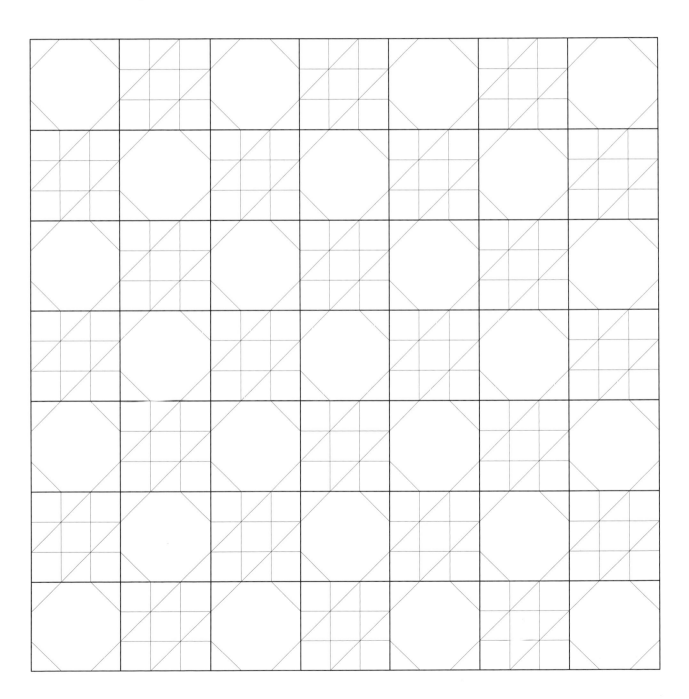

Marching Band in the Pines

Finished quilt size: 60" x 60"
Finished block size: 12" x 12"

Designed and pieced by Tammy Kelly. Machine quilted by Linda DeVries.

In this quilt, the dark Snowball block is surrounded by light corners, which creates a secondary star design when placed next to the Ohio Star block. This quilt goes together very quickly because of the large blocks and can be easily enlarged to make any size of bed quilt.

Fabric Selection Tips

I enjoy collecting fabric with a pinecone motif because the area where I live is surrounded by a ponderosa pine forest. The pinecone-bough print that I selected for the Snowball blocks has a black background, which complements but doesn't overpower the other colors. Any large-scale focus fabric would work well for the center of the block. Each Ohio Star block contains two various black fabrics, two different light fabrics, and a medium gold that was used for the corners. This selection forms a bold contrast so that the black stars really stand out. For variety, I used four different black fabrics for the stars. The medium gold corners fade into the background, yet still make a secondary design of star points. Fabrics with metallic gold stars, dots, and musical notes add elegance.

MATERIALS

Yardages are based on 42"-wide fabric.

1⅝ yards of black print for Snowball blocks

⅜ yard *each* of 4 assorted black prints for Ohio Star blocks

1¼ yards of light print A for blocks

1 yard of light print B for Ohio Star blocks

⅔ yard of gold fabric for Ohio Star blocks

⅝ yard of black print for binding

3¾ yards of fabric for backing

66" x 66" piece of batting

CUTTING

All measurements include ¼"-wide seam allowances.

From light print A, cut:

✦ 6 strips, 4½" x 42"; crosscut into 48 squares, 4½" x 4½"

✦ 2 strips, 5¼" x 42"; crosscut into 13 squares, 5¼" x 5¼". Cut each square twice diagonally to yield 52 quarter-square triangles.

From the black print for Snowball blocks, cut:

✦ 4 strips, 12½" x 42"; crosscut into 12 squares, 12½" x 12½"

From light print B, cut:

✦ 4 strips, 4⅞" x 42"; crosscut into 26 squares, 4⅞" x 4⅞". Cut each square once diagonally to yield 52 half-square triangles.

✦ 2 strips, 5¼" x 42"; crosscut into 13 squares, 5¼" x 5¼". Cut each square twice diagonally to yield 52 quarter-square triangles.

From the gold, cut:

✦ 4 strips, 4⅞" x 42"; crosscut into 26 squares, 4⅞" x 4⅞". Cut each square once diagonally to yield 52 half-square triangles.

From the 4 assorted black prints, cut a *total* of:

✦ 5 strips, 5¼" x 42"; crosscut into 13 sets of 2 squares (26 total), 5¼" x 5¼". Cut each set of squares twice diagonally to yield 8 quarter-square triangles (104 total). Keep the triangles from each set together.

✦ 13 squares, 4½" x 4½"

From the black print for binding, cut:

✦ 7 strips, 2½" x 42"

MAKING THE BLOCKS

1. To make the Snowball blocks, press the light print A 4½" squares in half diagonally, wrong sides together. Open each square and place one in each corner of a black print 12½" square as shown. Sew on the fold line of each corner square. Trim ¼" away from the seam using a rotary cutter and ruler to cut accurately. Set aside the cut-away triangle pairs for a future project. Press open the attached triangle in each corner to complete the Snowball block. The block should measure 12½" square. Repeat to make a total of 12 blocks.

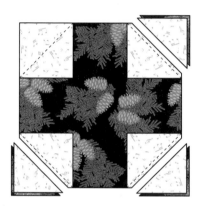

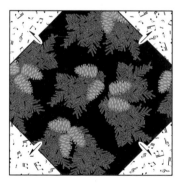

Make 12.

2. To make the Ohio Star blocks, refer to "Leftover Triangle Pairs" (page 11) to chain sew a light print B half-square triangle to each gold triangle to make half-square-triangle units. Press the seam allowances toward the gold fabric. Make 52 units.

Make 52.

3. Using one set of matching black print quarter-square triangles, chain sew four triangles to four light print B quarter-square triangles and the remaining four black print triangles to four light print A quarter-square triangles. Press the seam allowances toward the black fabric. Clip the triangles apart. Repeat with the remaining black print triangle sets to make 13 sets of joined triangles.

Make 13 sets of 4 (52 total).

4. Working with the joined triangles from one set, sew the joined triangles together as shown to make a quarter-square-triangle unit. Press the seam allowance in either direction. The unit should measure 4½". Repeat to make a total of 13 sets of four units (52 total).

Make 13 sets
of 4 (52 total).

5. Lay out four half-square-triangle units, four matching quarter-square-triangle units, and one black 4½" square (that is a different print than the quarter-square-triangle units) into three horizontal rows as shown. Sew the units in each row together. Press the seam allowances away from the quarter-square-triangle units. Sew the rows together, matching the seams. Press the seam allowances away from the center. Repeat to make a total of 13 blocks.

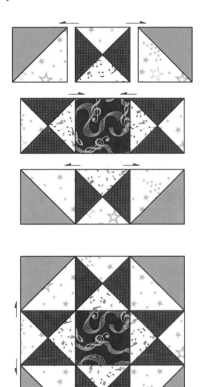

Make 13.

ASSEMBLING THE QUILT

1. Lay out the blocks in five horizontal rows of five blocks each. Alternate the blocks in each row and from row to row.

2. Sew the blocks in each row together. Press the seam allowances toward the Snowball blocks.

3. Sew the rows together. Press the seam allowances in one direction. Press the entire quilt top.

Quilt assembly

FINISHING THE QUILT

Refer to "Quilting Basics" (page 12) as needed to complete the following steps.

1. Layer the quilt top with the batting and backing. Baste the layers together.

2. Hand or machine quilt as desired.

3. Square up the quilt sandwich if needed.

4. Prepare and sew the binding to the quilt using the double-fold technique. Add a label.

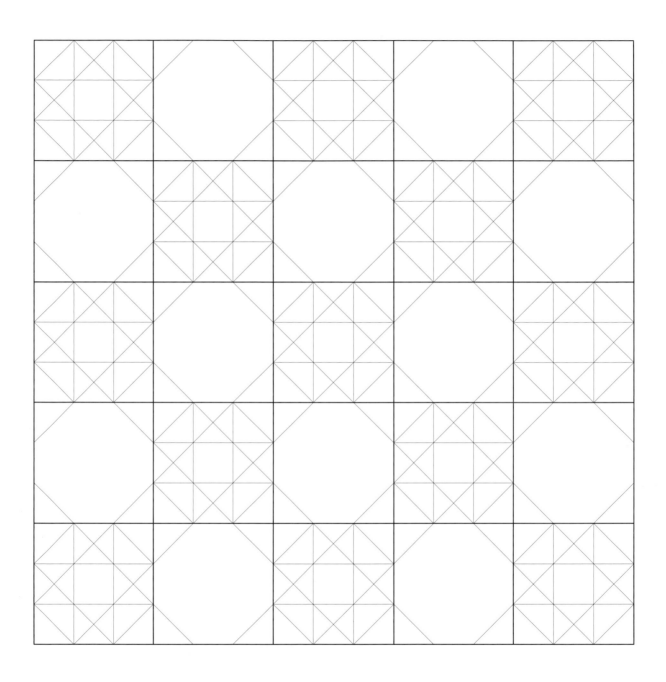

Wings of a Dragonfly

Finished quilt size: 30¼" x 30¼"
Finished block size: 5¾" x 5¾"

Designed and pieced by Tammy Kelly. Machine quilted by Linda DeVries.

This small wall hanging or table centerpiece, which can easily be sewn in a day, combines 5¾" Snowball blocks with Bright Hopes blocks. Almost any combination of light, medium, and dark fabrics will work for the quilt center.

Fabric Selection Tips

Almost like magic, when the appropriate-value fabrics are positioned correctly, a complex yet simple-to-make design is created. In this quilt, the lightest fabric is used as the background; the medium and dark fabrics create the rings. I chose to work with all batiks because I enjoy the variations in color on the fabrics. The light center of the Snowball block is an attractive place for an eye-catching or theme-related quilting design. The outer border fabric contains all the colors used in the quilt center.

MATERIALS

Yardages are based on 42"-wide fabric.

½ yard of purple print for outer border

½ yard of medium aqua print for blocks, partial blocks, and binding

⅜ yard of dark purple fabric for blocks, partial blocks, and corner units

⅓ yard of light blue fabric for blocks, partial blocks, and corner units

¼ yard of medium blue fabric for inner border

¼ yard of medium purple fabric for middle border

1⅛ yards of fabric for backing

37" x 37" piece of batting

CUTTING

All measurements include ¼"-wide seam allowances.

From the medium aqua print, cut:
- ✦ 3 strips, 2½" x 42"; crosscut into:
  - • 24 squares, 2½" x 2½"
  - • 8 rectangles, 2½" x 4¼"
- ✦ 4 strips, 1½" x 42"

From the dark purple, cut:
- ✦ 3 strips, 2½" x 42"; crosscut into:
  - • 12 squares, 2½" x 2½"
  - • 16 rectangles, 2½" x 4¼"
- ✦ 2 squares, 2⅞" x 2⅞"; cut once diagonally to yield 4 triangles

From the light blue, cut:
- ✦ 1 strip, 6¼" x 42"; crosscut into 5 squares, 6¼" x 6¼"
- ✦ 1 strip, 2½" x 26"; crosscut into 4 rectangles, 2½" x 6¼"
- ✦ 2 squares, 2⅞" x 2⅞"; cut once diagonally to yield 4 triangles
- ✦ 4 squares, 2¼" x 2¼"

From the medium blue, cut:
- ✦ 2 strips, 1¼" x 21¾"
- ✦ 2 strips, 1¼" x 23¼"

From the medium purple, cut:
- ✦ 2 strips, 1" x 23¼"
- ✦ 2 strips, 1" x 24¼"

From the purple print, cut:
- ✦ 2 strips, 3¾" x 24¼"
- ✦ 2 strips, 3¾" x 30¾"

MAKING THE BLOCKS

1. To make the Snowball blocks, press 16 of the medium aqua 2½" squares and 4 of the dark purple 2½" squares in half diagonally, wrong sides together. Open each square and place one aqua square in each corner of a light blue 6¼" square as shown. Sew on the fold line of each corner square. Trim ¼" away from the seam using a rotary cutter and ruler to cut accurately. Set aside the cut-away triangle pairs for a future project. Press open the attached triangle in each corner to complete the Snowball block. The block should measure 6¼" square. Make a total of four blocks with medium aqua corners and one block with dark purple corners.

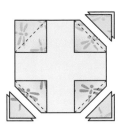
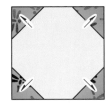

Make 4.

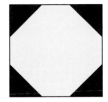

Make 1.

2. To make the Bright Hopes blocks, place a light blue 2¼" square along the bottom right corner of a medium aqua 2½" x 4¼" rectangle, right sides together. Sew the pieces together, stopping at the center of the square. Finger-press the seam allowance away from the square. Sew a dark purple rectangle to the right side of this unit. Finger-press the seam allowance away from the square. Add a medium aqua rectangle along the bottom edge of the unit. Finger-press the seam allowance away from the square. Sew a dark purple rectangle along the lower-left side of the unit, keeping the first aqua rectangle out of the way. Finger-press the seam allowance away from the square. Sew the remaining portion of the seam of the first medium aqua rectangle to complete the

block. Repeat to make a total of four blocks, making sure each block is sewn together in the same order.

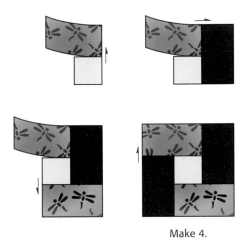

Make 4.

ASSEMBLING THE PARTIAL BLOCKS AND CORNER UNITS

1. Press the remaining dark purple squares in half diagonally, wrong sides together. Open each square and place them on opposite corners of a light blue rectangle as shown. Sew on the fold line of each corner square. Trim ¼" away from the seam using a rotary cutter and ruler. Set aside the cut-away triangle pairs for a future project. Press open the attached triangle in each corner. Repeat to make a total of four partial Snowball blocks.

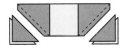

Make 4.

2. Sew a medium aqua square to a dark purple rectangle. Press the seam allowance toward the rectangle. Repeat to make a total of eight partial Bright Hopes blocks.

Make 8.

3. Sew a dark purple triangle to a light blue triangle as shown. Press the seam allowance toward the purple fabric. Repeat to make a total of four corner units.

Make 4.

ASSEMBLING THE QUILT CENTER

1. Lay out the blocks, partial blocks, and corner units in five horizontal rows. Check the layout for accuracy.

2. Sew the pieces in each row together. Press the seam allowances away from the Snowball blocks and partial Snowball blocks.

3. Sew the rows together. Press the seam allowances in one direction. Press the entire quilt center. The pieced quilt center should measure 21¾" square.

ADDING THE BORDERS

1. Sew the medium blue 1¼" x 21¾" strips to the sides of the quilt center. Press the seam allowances toward the borders. Sew the medium blue 1¼" x 23¼" strips to the top and bottom of the quilt center.

2. Repeat step 1 with the medium purple strips and then the purple print strips to add the middle and outer borders to the quilt top, sewing the shorter strips to the sides and the longer strips to the top and bottom. After you attach each strip, press the seam allowances toward the border strip you just added.

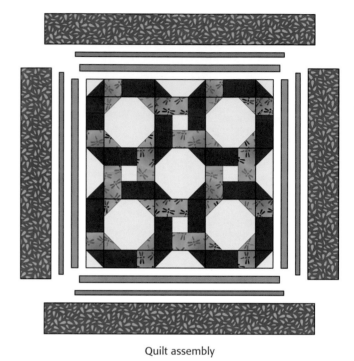

Quilt assembly

FINISHING THE QUILT

Refer to "Quilting Basics" (page 12) as needed to complete the following steps.

1. Layer the quilt top with the batting and backing. Baste the layers together.

2. Hand or machine quilt as desired.

3. Square up the quilt sandwich if needed.

4. Prepare and sew the binding to the quilt using the single-fold technique. Add a label.

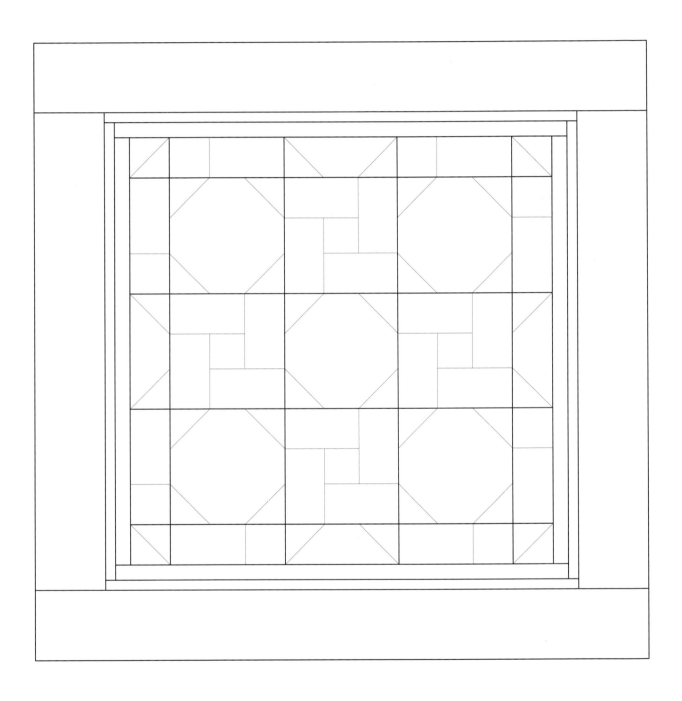

Ring around the Posies

Finished quilt size: 71¾" x 94¾"
Finished block size: 5¾" x 5¾"

Designed and pieced by Tammy Kelly. Hand quilted by Loralie Martin.

This visually stimulating scrappy quilt combines the Snowball block with the Bright Hopes block, creating a twin-size version of "Wings of a Dragonfly" (page 51). Attractive pinwheels in the borders are made from the leftover corners of the Snowball blocks.

Fabric Selection Tips

The rose-colored fabric with white and green circles inspired this quilt design. I carefully selected a variety of fabrics from medium pink to dark burgundy, and then added an assortment of medium greens to create the rings that form when the Snowball blocks and Bright Hopes blocks are combined. The block centers are made from a frosty white fabric. Various-sized borders frame the quilt, drawing the eye to the center and complementing the overall design. The widest border, made from subtly checked khaki green, contrasts nicely with the pinwheel blocks.

MATERIALS

Yardages are based on 42"-wide fabric.

2⅝ yards of white fabric for blocks

¼ yard *each* of 9 assorted medium green prints for blocks, partial blocks, and corner units

¼ yard *each* of 8 assorted medium to dark rose-colored prints for blocks and partial blocks

1⅜ yards of khaki-colored check for third border

⅞ yard of dark green fabric for first and fifth borders

½ yard of dark rose fabric for second and fourth borders

¾ yard of rose print for binding

6¼ yards of fabric for backing

78" x 101" piece of batting

CUTTING

All measurements include ¼"-wide seam allowances.

From the assorted rose prints, cut a *total* of:
- ✦ 24 strips, 2½" x 42"; crosscut into:
  - • 164 squares, 2½" x 2½"
  - • 116 rectangles, 2½" x 4¼"

From the assorted green prints, cut a *total* of:
- ✦ 25 strips, 2½" x 42"; crosscut into:
  - • 136 squares, 2½" x 2½"
  - • 140 rectangles, 2½" x 4¼"
- ✦ 2 squares, 2⅞" x 2⅞"; cut once diagonally to yield 4 triangles

From the white, cut:
- ✦ 10 strips, 6¼" x 42"; crosscut into 59 squares, 6¼" x 6¼"
- ✦ 4 strips, 2¼" x 42"; crosscut into 58 squares, 2¼" x 2¼"
- ✦ 4 strips, 2½" x 42"; crosscut into 20 rectangles, 2½" x 6¼"
- ✦ 2 squares, 2⅞" x 2⅞"; cut once diagonally to yield 4 triangles

From the dark green, cut:
- ✦ 16 strips, 1½" x 42"

From the dark rose, cut:
- ✦ 15 strips, 1" x 42"

From the khaki-colored check, cut:
- ✦ 8 strips, 5½" x 42"; crosscut into:
  - • 4 pieces, 5½" x 38⅞"
  - • 4 pieces, 5½" x 27⅜"

From the rose print for binding, cut:
- ✦ 9 strips, 2½" x 42"

MAKING THE BLOCKS

1. To make the Snowball blocks, press 140 of the assorted rose 2½" squares and 96 of the assorted green 2½" squares in half diagonally, wrong sides together. Open each square and place one rose square in each corner of a white 6¼" square as shown. Sew on the fold line of each corner square. Trim ¼" away from the seam using a rotary cutter and ruler to cut accurately. Set aside the cut-away triangle pairs for the border Pinwheel blocks. Press open the attached triangle in each corner to complete the Snowball block. The block should measure 6¼" square. Make a total of 35 blocks with rose corners. Repeat with the green squares to make a total of 24 blocks with green corners.

Make 35.

Make 24.

2. To make the Bright Hopes blocks, place a white 2¼" square along the bottom-right corner of an assorted green 2½" x 4¼" rectangle, right sides together. Sew the pieces together, stopping at the center of the square. Finger-press the seam allowance away from the square. Sew a rose print rectangle to the right side of this unit. Finger-press the seam allowance away from the square. Add a different green rectangle along the bottom edge of the unit. Finger-press the seam allowance away from the square. Sew a different rose print rectangle along the lower-left side of the unit, keeping the first green rectangle out of the way. Finger-press the seam allowance away from the square. Sew the remaining portion of the seam of the first green rectangle to complete the block.

Repeat to make a total of 58 blocks, making sure each block is sewn together in the same order.

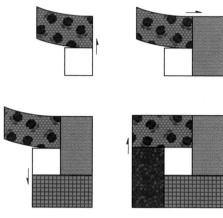

Make 58.

ASSEMBLING THE PARTIAL BLOCKS AND CORNER UNITS

1. Press the remaining assorted green squares in half diagonally, wrong sides together. Open each square and place one on opposite corners of a white rectangle as shown. Sew on the fold line of each corner square. Trim ¼" away from the seam using a rotary cutter and ruler. Set aside the cut-away triangle pairs for a future project. Press open the attached triangle in each corner. Repeat to make a total of 20 partial Snowball blocks.

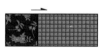

Make 20.

2. Sew a rose square to a green rectangle as shown. Press the seam allowance toward the rectangle. Repeat to make a total of 24 partial Bright Hopes blocks.

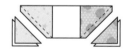

Make 24.

3. Sew a green triangle to a white triangle as shown. Press the seam allowance toward the green fabric. Repeat to make a total of four corner units.

Make 4.

ASSEMBLING THE QUILT CENTER

1. Lay out the blocks, partial blocks, and corner units in 15 horizontal rows. Check the layout for accuracy.

2. Sew the pieces in each row together. Press the seam allowances away from the Snowball blocks and partial Snowball blocks.

3. Sew the rows together. Press the seam allowances in one direction. Press the entire quilt center. The pieced quilt center should measure 56¼" x 79¼".

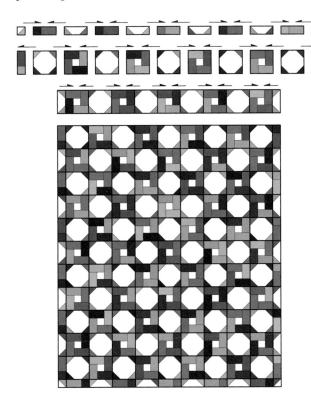

ASSEMBLING THE BORDER PINWHEEL BLOCKS

1. From the triangle pairs that were set aside after trimming the corners of the Snowball blocks, select eight sets of eight matching green pairs and eight sets of eight matching rose pairs.

2. Refer to "Leftover Triangle Pairs" (page 11) to chain sew the pairs of triangles together to make 64 green and 64 rose half-square-triangle units. Press the seam allowances toward the green or rose fabrics. Use a ruler and rotary cutter to trim each unit to 1¾" square.

Make 8
sets of 8
(64 total).   Make 8
sets of 8
(64 total).

3. Sew two matching green half-square-triangle units together as shown. Repeat with the remaining green units. Press all the seam allowances in the same direction.

Make 8
sets of 4
(32 total).

4. Sew two matching rose half-square-triangle units together as shown. Repeat with the remaining rose units. Press all the seam allowances in the opposite direction from the green units.

Make 8
sets of 4
(32 total).

5. Sew a green unit to a rose unit as shown. Press the seam allowances in one direction. Repeat with the remaining green and rose units.

Make 8
sets of 4
(32 total).

6. Sew the four units from one set together as shown to complete a Pinwheel block. Press the seam allowances as indicated. Repeat to make a total of eight blocks. The blocks should measure 5½" square.

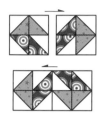

Make 8.

ASSEMBLING AND ADDING THE BORDERS

1. Piece together the dark green 1½" x 42" strips end to end. Repeat with the dark rose 1" x 42" strips.

2. For the first border, from the pieced dark green strip cut two strips 79¼" long for the side borders and two strips 58¼" long for the top and bottom borders. Set aside the remainder of the strip. Sew the side borders to the quilt center. Press the seam allowances toward the borders. Sew the top and bottom borders to the quilt center. Press the seam allowances toward the borders.

3. For the second border, from the pieced dark rose strip cut two strips 81¼" long for the side borders and two strips 59¼" long for the top and bottom borders. Set aside the remainder of the strip. Sew the borders to the quilt in the same manner as for the first border. Press the seam allowances toward the second border.

4. For the third pieced border, sew a khaki-colored check 5½" x 38⅞" piece to each side of a Pinwheel block to make a side border. Make two. Sew a green check 5½" x 27⅜" piece to each side of a Pinwheel block. Sew a Pinwheel block to each end of the strip to make a top or bottom border. Make two. Sew the borders to the quilt in the same manner as the previous borders. Press the seam allowances toward the third border.

5. For the fourth border, from the remainder of the pieced dark rose strip cut two strips 92¼" long for the side borders and two strips 70¼" long for the top

and bottom borders. Add the borders to the quilt in the same manner as the previous borders. Press the seam allowances toward the fourth border.

6. For the fifth border, from the remainder of the pieced dark green strip cut two strips 93¼" long for the side borders and two strips 72¼" long for the top and bottom borders. Add the borders to the quilt in the same manner as the previous borders. Press the seam allowances toward the fifth border.

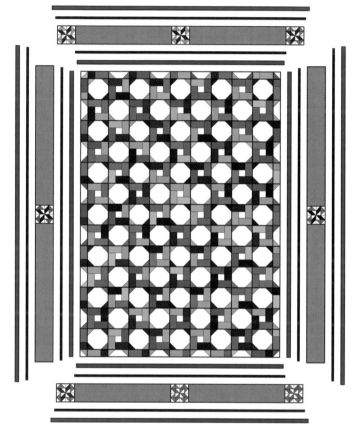

Quilt assembly

FINISHING THE QUILT

Refer to "Quilting Basics" (page 12) as needed to complete the following steps.

1. Layer the quilt top with the batting and backing. Baste the layers together.

2. Hand or machine quilt as desired.

3. Square up the quilt sandwich if needed.

4. Prepare and sew the binding to the quilt using the double-fold technique. Add a label.

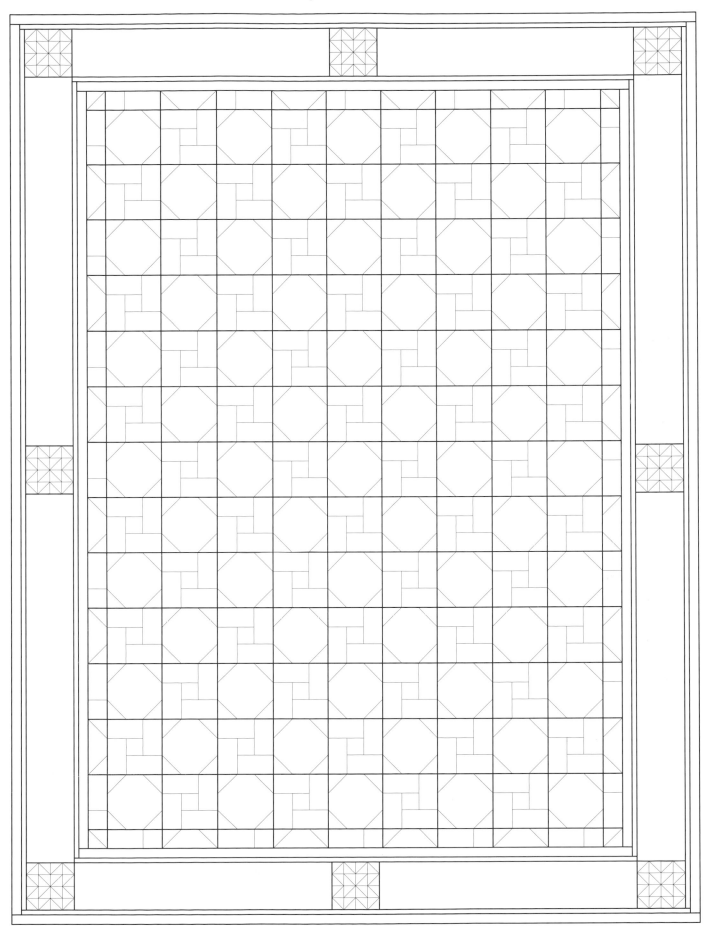

Resources

Batting
Quilter's Dream Batting
589 Central Dr.
Virginia Beach, VA 23454
888-268-8664
www.quiltersdreambatting.com

Computer Printer Fabric
June Tailor
P.O. Box 208
2861 Hwy. 175
Richfield, WI 53076
800-844-5400
www.junetailor.com

Pigma Micron Pens
Sakura of America
30780 San Clemente St.
Hayward, CA 94544
800-776-6257
www.sakuraofamerica.com

About the Author

Tammy Kelly is a quilt designer, teacher, and author. She teaches quilting at regional quilt shops, her local community college, and at quilt camps. She uses all her experience as an elementary school teacher when planning and conducting a quilt class. She also encourages her students to be creative with fabric selection and design.

Tammy's favorite quilting topic is COLOR! The fabric "talks" to her, and she carefully chooses just the right color combination for each individual quilt. Exploring patterns and color values are her passion. Her favorite quilt is always the next one—the one that is yet to be created. She never runs out of ideas, creativity, or inspiration.

Many of her quilts have been published in national quilting magazines. She also self-publishes her own pattern line called Common Threads. *Snowball Quilts* is her second book.

Living in the beautiful mountain town of Flagstaff, Arizona, provides many opportunities for Tammy; her husband, Dave; and daughter, Lynnae, to enjoy entertaining friends, trying new recipes, and hiking.

New and Bestselling Titles from

America's Best-Loved Craft & Hobby Books
America's Best-Loved Knitting Books

America's Best-Loved Quilt Books

NEW RELEASES
Adoration Quilts
Better by the Dozen
Blessed Home Quilt, The
Hooked on Wool
It's a Wrap
Let's Quilt!
Origami Quilts
Over Easy
Primitive Gatherings
Quilt Revival
Sew One and You're Done
Scraps of Time
Simple Chenille Quilts
Simple Traditions
Simply Primitive
Surprisingly Simple Quilts
Two-Block Theme Quilts
Wheel of Mystery Quilts

APPLIQUÉ
Appliqué Takes Wing
Easy Appliqué Samplers
Garden Party
Raise the Roof
Stitch and Split Appliqué
Tea in the Garden

LEARNING TO QUILT
Happy Endings, Revised Edition
Loving Stitches, Revised Edition
Magic of Quiltmaking, The
Quilter's Quick Reference Guide, The
Your First Quilt Book (or it should be!)

PAPER PIECING
40 Bright and Bold Paper-Pieced Blocks
50 Fabulous Paper-Pieced Stars
300 Paper-Pieced Quilt Blocks
Easy Machine Paper Piecing
Quilt Block Bonanza
Quilter's Ark, A
Show Me How to Paper Piece

PIECING
40 Fabulous Quick-Cut Quilts
101 Fabulous Rotary-Cut Quilts
365 Quilt Blocks a Year: Perpetual
   Calendar
1000 Great Quilt Blocks
Big 'n Easy
Clever Quilts Encore
Once More around the Block
Stack a New Deck

QUILTS FOR BABIES & CHILDREN
American Doll Quilts
Even More Quilts for Baby
More Quilts for Baby
Quilts for Baby
Sweet and Simple Baby Quilts

SCRAP QUILTS
More Nickel Quilts
Nickel Quilts
Save the Scraps
Successful Scrap Quilts
   from Simple Rectangles
Treasury of Scrap Quilts, A

TOPICS IN QUILTMAKING
Alphabet Soup
Cottage-Style Quilts
Creating Your Perfect Quilting Space
Focus on Florals
Follow the Dots . . . to Dazzling Quilts
More Biblical Quilt Blocks
Scatter Garden Quilts
Sensational Sashiko
Warm Up to Wool

CRAFTS
Bag Boutique
Purely Primitive
Scrapbooking Off the Page…and on the
   Wall
Stamp in Color
Vintage Workshop, The: Gifts for All
   Occasions

KNITTING & CROCHET
200 Knitted Blocks
365 Knitting Stitches a Year: Perpetual
   Calendar
Crochet from the Heart
First Crochet
First Knits
Fun and Funky Crochet
Handknit Style
Knits from the Heart
Little Box of Knitted Ponchos and Wraps,
   The
Little Box of Knitted Throws, The
Little Box of Crocheted Hats and Scarves,
   The
Little Box of Scarves, The
Little Box of Scarves II, The
Little Box of Sweaters, The
Pursenalities
Sensational Knitted Socks

Our books are available at bookstores and your favorite craft,
fabric, and yarn retailers. If you don't see the title
you're looking for, visit us at
www.martingale-pub.com
or contact us at:

1-800-426-3126

International: 1-425-483-3313 **Fax:** 1-425-486-7596
Email: info@martingale-pub.com

05/06